Napa Valley and Sonoma

Intelligent Guides to Wines & Top Vineyards

Benjamin Lewin MW

Copyright © 2016 Benjamin Lewin

Vendange Press

ISBN-13: 978-1535507684

www.vendangepress.com

This guide covers the North Coast of California. The greatest focus is on Napa Valley, but I also include Sonoma Valley and two areas to the south of San Francisco: the Santa Cruz Mountains and Mount Harlan. The first part discusses the regions and their wines; the second part has individual profiles of the top producers, showing how each winemaker interprets that character.

In the first part I address the nature of the wines made today and ask how this has changed, how it's driven by tradition or competition, and how styles may evolve in the future. I show how the wines are related to the terroir and to the types of grape varieties that are grown, and I explain the classification system. For each region, I suggest reference wines that I believe typify the area; in some cases, where there is a split between, for example, modernists and traditionalists, there may be wines from each camp.

There's no single definition for what constitutes a top producer. Leading producers range from those who are so prominent as to represent the common public face of an appellation to those who demonstrate an unexpected potential on a tiny scale. The producers profiled in the guide should represent the best of both tradition and innovation in wine in the region

In the profiles, I have tried to give a sense of each producer's aims for his wines, of the personality and philosophy behind them—to meet the person who makes the wine, as it were, as much as to review the wines themselves. For each producer I suggest reference wines that are a good starting point for understanding his style. Most of the producers welcome visits, although some require appointments: details are in the profiles.

The guide is based on many visits to Napa and its associated regions over recent years. I owe an enormous debt to the many producers who cooperated in this venture by engaging in discussion and opening innumerable bottles for tasting. This guide would not have been possible without them.

How to read the producer profiles

The second part of this guide consists of profiles of individual wine producers. Each profile shows a sample label, a picture of the winery, and details of production, followed by a description of the producer and winemaker. The producer's rating (from one to four stars) is shown to the right of the name.

The profiles are organized geographically, and each group of profiles is preceded by a map showing the locations of starred producers to help plan itineraries.

A full list of the symbols used in the profiles appears at the start of the profile section. This is an example of a profile:

Hospices de Beaune

Hospices de Beaune

VOLNAY
Premier Cru
Appellation Volnay Contrôlée
Cuvée Blondeau

Mis en bouteille par
Jean-Luc Aegerter
Négociant-Eleveur à 21900 Nuits-Saint-Georges

13 % vol.   Produit de France   750 ml

Hotel Dieu, Beaune, France
address

03 80 24 44 02

Catherine Guillemot

catherine.guillemot@ch-beaune.fr

Corton *principal appellation*

Napa Valley, Cabernet Sauvignon
red reference wine

Sonoma Valley, Chardonnay
white reference wine

www.hospices-de-beaune.com

details of producer
60 ha; 400,000 bottles
vineyards & production

The Hospices de Beaune was founded in 1443 by Nicolas Rolin, chancellor of Burgundy, as a hospital for the poor. Standing in the heart of Beaune, the original buildings of the Hotel Dieu, now converted into a museum, surround a courtyard where an annual auction of wines was first held in 1859. The wines come from vineyards held as part of the endowment of the Hospices, and are sold in November to negociants who then take possession of the barrels and mature the wines in their own styles. (Today the auction is held in the modern covered marketplace opposite the Hotel Dieu.) There are 45 cuvées (32 red and 13 white); most come from premier or grand crus from the Côte de Beaune or Côte de Nuits, but because holdings are small (depending on past donations of land to the Hospices) many cuvées consist of blends from different crus (and are identified by brand names). The vines are cultivated, and the wine is made, by the Hospices. For some years the vineyards of the Hospices were not tended as carefully as they might have been, and the winemaking was less than perfect, but the appointment of a new régisseur has led to improvements in the present century. The name of the Hospices is only a starting point, because each negociant stamps his own style on the barriques he buys.

Contents

Napa Valley

Napa Valley has been at the very heart of the rise of New World wines. Until the famous Judgment of Paris tasting in 1976, when Cabernet Sauvignon and Chardonnay from Napa Valley placed ahead of Bordeaux and Burgundy, there was very little interest in wines from outside Europe. The situation then changed dramatically, and not only was Napa Valley, and in due course other places in the New World, taken seriously, but the move began to consider wines in terms of single grape varieties. Yet at the the time, there were few inklings in Napa that their wines were about to play a major part on the world stage.

The news of the tasting came as a shock in Napa. The immediate effect was to sell out the wines that had won—the Chateau Montelena Chardonnay and Stag's Leap Cabernet. But the more important, longer term effect was to validate the concept of high-end wines from Napa. Bo Barrett of Chateau Montelena recollects that up to then, it had been an uphill battle to get the wines into distribution on the East Coast. "The practical consequence was that distributors would take the wines," he says. The effect on style was to reinforce the view that Napa should compete with Bordeaux. "The Paris tasting had the effect that if we won there, we must be as good, and we should make wine more like Bordeaux," says Fred Schrader.

Attempts to produce wine in California go back for more than a century. At the start of the twentieth century, wine labeled as "Claret" was more than half of production, and Zinfandel accounted for another third. White wine, in the form of "Riesling" was less than 10%. When the idiocy of Prohibition was introduced in 1920, California had 40,000 hectares of vineyards and was producing the equivalent of about 20 million cases of wine annually. The most common plantings were Zinfandel, Carignan, Mourvèdre, Grenache, and Durif (Petite Syrah). Production of dry table wine was a bit greater than production of fortified (sweet) wine. At the end of Prohibition, Zinfandel, Alicante, and Carignan were two thirds of plantings in California. White varieties had disappeared. The trend towards mass production varieties continued for the next half century.

Napa Valley was a mixture of vineyards and prune orchards at the start of the twentieth century. Many of today's vineyards were planted in place of prune orchards.

After the adjustment to home winemaking during Prohibition, popular taste favored sweet wines, and California adjusted to the new market, in which fortified wines outsold dry wines by three to one. It was to take 40 years to reverse the trend. A huge proportion of wine was sold as an alternative to spirits at the very low end, and became known as the "Skid Row Trade." When the move to quality started in the 1970s, bulk production varieties altogether accounted for more than 80% of all production. Cabernet Sauvignon was only 5%. In whites, Colombard (not a variety usually associated with quality) was the major variety with 40% of plantings. Today, Bordeaux varieties account for 80% of black plantings, and Chardonnay accounts for almost 70% of white plantings.

Some date the modern era in Napa from 1966, when Robert Mondavi opened his winery, the first new winery to be built in Napa since Prohibition. New wineries have been the driving force in Napa's revival: three quarters of Napa's current 400 wineries have been established since 1966, and it's a striking measure of change that you can count on the fingers of one hand the number of producers profiled in this guide who even existed in 1970.

Napa Valley is now a monoculture of vines all the way across the valley floor.

Grape Varieties in Napa

Today Napa Valley is closely associated with Cabernet Sauvignon, but Cabernet Sauvignon production was almost insignificant in Napa Valley until the 1970s, and it was not necessarily obvious that it would be the grape of the future. Asked whether Cabernet Sauvignon was the obvious variety of choice when Joseph Phelps was established in 1973, Bill Phelps says, "Hardly. The first three years Riesling was the main variety. It wasn't clear Cabernet would be the future until the late seventies. At the start we planted Riesling, Pinot Noir, and Cabernet Sauvignon. During the 1980s we realized we couldn't do every variety and we focused on Cabernet Sauvignon."

As it became clear that Cabernet Sauvignon should be the black grape of choice, what were the producers' stylistic aims? When you decided on Cabernet, were you trying to compete with

Bordeaux, I asked Bill Phelps? "Absolutely. The model was the first vintage of Insignia in 1974. Joe made it like a Bordeaux and really wanted it to be a blend. In fact, the second vintage was 80% Merlot." It has since settled down to be a Cabernet-dominated blend, typically with around 80% Cabernet Sauvignon. Have objectives changed since the first vintage? "Our style has changed. This was a decision. As Napa came into its own, we realized what was in the material and we could rely on the vineyards. In the 1970s, things were driven by winemaking, now they are more driven by what happens in the vineyards. There's still a strong affinity with Bordeaux, but now we have established our own identity."

Once Cabernet Sauvignon was established as the principal grape, if it was blended with other varieties in Napa, they were the usual suspects: Merlot, Cabernet Franc, and Petit Verdot. A split between those who believe that pure Cabernet Sauvignon gives the best results and those who believe in the sanctity of blending continues to this day.

Wines labeled as Cabernet Sauvignon are allowed to include 15% of other varieties in most New World countries, and up to 25% in the United States, so it would be a fine line to distinguish them from blends dominated by Cabernet Sauvignon. In Napa, there's a large proportion of wines labeled as Cabernet Sauvignon that are just over the 75% limit.

Varietal-labeled Cabernet Sauvignon is Napa's main challenge to Bordeaux, but there is another option for producers who want to include more than 25% of other varieties. The Meritage category was introduced in 1988 by a group of producers to describe wines based on a Bordeaux blend. The wines are usually dominated by Cabernet Sauvignon but may also include Merlot, Cabernet Franc, Petit Verdot, and Malbec, Meritage has few restrictions on the exact blend, and perhaps for this reason has not really impacted the mainstream. In fact, it seems to be disappearing. There are also wines that are described simply as "proprietary reds," and which can contain any mix of varieties, but which usually have Cabernet Sauvignon as the most important variety.

Chardonnay has taken over as Napa's main white representative, and Sauvignon Blanc has become firmly established in second place. Both tend to show rich styles, but this is most evident for Sauvignon Blanc, especially when it is vinified in the Fumé Blanc

Napa Valley is north of San Pablo Bay, an hour from San Francisco.

style pioneered by Robert Mondavi, using barrel fermentation in oak (sometimes new oak, at that). Both Chardonnay and Sauvignon Blanc are usually vinified to make single varietal wines.

New World Style

Napa's view on the appropriate style for Cabernet Sauvignon has evolved. As Napa began its revival, the general view was that Bordeaux was about elegance, and California was about power. Initially Napa Valley set out to compete with Bordeaux, but by the 1990s came around to the view that the wine should be in a richer style more reflecting its warmer climate. This has been the basis of a continuing debate as to whether Cabernet Sauvignon (and for that matter wines based on other varieties) should reflect the character of the places where they originated in Europe, or should show a more "international" style reflecting the new places where they are made.

Fred Schrader, who has been associated with cult wines since the early nineties, thinks the change in style is an appropriate reflection of conditions in Napa. "In the mid eighties, people wanted to make wine just like Bordeaux. I was never part of that school, my attitude was why do we care? The climate and actually the seasons here are different. We have a hotter climate, with riper berries; we are more fruit forward. We should not try to emulate, we should try to make something that reflects who we are." Anthony Bell dates a deliberate change to riper styles from the early nineties, and attributes it to Robert Parker's influence. "When I was running Beaulieu, by the late eighties, we were trying to change the style of our wines. By the mid nineties we were in our stride. Probably the period from 1990-1995 was when things changed." Anthony quotes a telling example of the change in style. "Today the reserve wines are made from grapes picked at the end of the season, but when I joined BV the Reserve was made from grapes picked first—because they came from the healthy vineyards that gave the best quality grapes."

The move to the riper, more "international" style was partly driven by critics who scored the wines highly—or perhaps more to the point, scored restrained wines poorly. Certainly attempts at a European aesthetic in Napa were criticized. There was a long-running difference of opinion between Mondavi and the *Wine Spectator* over style. The *Spectator's* lead critic on California, James Laube, commented in July 2001, "At a time when California's best winemakers are aiming for ripe, richer, more expressive wines, Mondavi appears headed in the opposite direction... [Winemaker] Tim Mondavi and I have different taste preferences... He has never concealed his distaste for big, ultra rich plush or tannic red wines. I know he can make rich, compelling wines, yet he prefers structured wines with elegance and finesse... the attempt to give his wines more nerve and backbone has come at the expense of body and texture... he's decided to turn his back on a climate ideally suited for producing ripe, dramatic wines, and rein in those qualities so that the wines show restraint rather than opulence." Tim Mondavi replied, "I am concerned... that while global wine quality has improved tremendously, there appears to be a current trend toward aggressively over-ripe, high in alcohol, over-oaked wines that are designed to stand out at a huge tasting rather than fulfill the more appropriate purpose of enhancing a meal."

There you have the whole debate in a nutshell. It's hard to defy the rush to ripeness: the price is likely to be lack of critical acclaim. Over recent decades, the story of Cabernet Sauvignon in Napa has been the struggle to control its ripeness.

Fog in Napa Valley

Napa Valley itself is really quite a confined area. About 30 miles long and generally less than a mile wide, it nestles between the Mayacamas mountains to the west (separating Napa from Sonoma) and the Vaca mountains to the east. Looking across the valley, a difference is immediately apparent between the Mayacamas Mountains, which are covered in vegetation, and the Vaca Mountains, which have a distinctly scrubby appearance. Weather comes from the Pacific, and the east is drier than the west, because rainfall gets blocked by the Mayacamas Mountains.

Fog rolls into Napa Valley from the Pacific most mornings, and disperses around midday.

The Mayacamas Mountains to the west are covered in evergreens.

Napa Valley has an abundance of that surprising key feature for wine production in California: fog. This is not usually welcome in wine-producing regions, but the climate in California would normally be too warm for fine wine production, and is rescued only by the regularity of the cooling fog. Almost all the top regions for wine production are in valleys that are cooled by fog rolling in from the Pacific Ocean. (The exceptions are vineyards at high enough elevations that cooling comes from the altitude.) Morning fog is fairly reliable in Napa, usually clearing around midday.

Because a high pressure system settles over the California coast each summer, the growing season tends to be warm and dry. Except for the absence of rain in the summer, the climate is perfect for agriculture. Irrigation fills the gap. The climate in Napa Valley escapes the European rule that temperatures become warmer going south; the northern end is decidedly warmer than the southern end, because the more open southern end gets cooling breezes from San Pablo bay, whereas the narrow northern end is effectively closed. At the very southern end, Napa itself is close in temperature to Bordeaux; but Calistoga at the far north is more like the south of

The hills to the east are dry and scrubby.

France, and it becomes too hot to grow Cabernet Sauvignon on the valley floor.

The collision between the three tectonic plates that created the valley some 150 million years ago left detritus of a great variety of soil types, with more than 40 different soil series classified in Napa. A major factor is the consistent difference between the warmer, and more fertile, valley floor, and the cooler terrain of the slopes to the west and the east. And moving from south to north, the soil changes from sediments deposited by past oceans to a more volcanic terrain, which also is prevalent on the mountains.

Climate and Terroir

Definition of individual regions, or more specifically identification of those locations where particular varieties grow best, developed slowly after the growth of the 1960s. The spur for the realization that not all sites in Napa Valley were created equal was the definition by University of California professors Albert Winkler

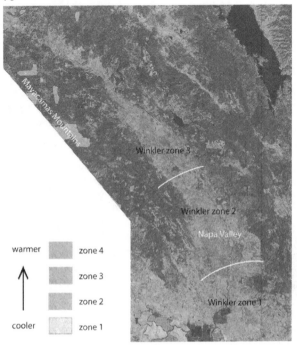

Climate mapping by Winkler originally divided the valley into three zones going from south to north. More recent data suggest the main difference is between the valley floor and the slopes and mountains on either side. Zones are defined in terms of degree days (a calculation of time above the minimum growing temperature for the grapevine).

and Maynard Amerine in the 1940s of heat zones in Napa Valley. Classifying California into five zones according to average temperatures during the growing season, they recommended suitable grape varieties for each region. Among the varieties recommended for the cooler, southern part of Napa Valley were Cabernet Sauvignon and Chardonnay, but it was not until the 1960s that growers paid much attention.

With the extension of grape growing from the valley floor (where it resumed after Prohibition) to the mountain slopes (planted after the revival of the seventies), there is considerable variation not only of terroir but also of climate. In fact, the most important determinant of climate may be elevation, rather than position along the valley. The original definition of heat zones mapped Napa into three zones, with the Carneros region at the southern end the coolest in zone 1, Napa itself in zone 2, but Oakville and St. Helena in warmer zone 3. More recent data confirm a gradual increase in average growing season temperatures going up the valley, but put the whole valley floor into zone 4, with conditions becoming significantly cooler moving up in elevation into the mountains on either side.

To the casual tourist—of whom there are more than five million annually—driving up Route 29 on the western side, or back down the Silverado trail on the eastern side, Napa Valley might appear quite homogeneous, a veritable sea of vines stretching across the valley between the mountains on either side. The land appears flat until close to the mountains. Taking any cross street between the two highways, you travel exclusively through vineyards. The Napa river in the center of the valley seems unimportant. The impression of dense plantation is true for the center of the valley, where three quarters of the land is planted with vines, but this apparent consistency is somewhat deceptive.

The heart of the valley is characterized by alluvial fans, formed by streams that flowed out of the mountains. When a stream opens out on to a valley floor, it deposits sediment as it flows. Over time, the sediment causes the watercourse to shift sideways, creating a fan-like area of sediment. Alluvial fans run continuously along the west side of the valley; the series is more broken up along the east side. Known locally as "benches," the most famous are the Oakville Bench and the Rutherford Bench, where production of fine wine started in the nineteenth century. (Valley floor tends to be used in two senses in Napa. Generally used as generic description to distinguish terrain between the mountain ranges as opposed to the actual slopes, it is not pejorative. Sometimes it is used more disparagingly to distinguish fertile soils from the alluvial fans.) Sediments become finer, and the soils that form on them become richer, as an alluvial fan widens out. Beyond the fan, soils on a valley floor can be too rich for producing fine wine.

"Terroir isn't everywhere. In fact, terroir is in very few places. I have five wines and one is a terroir wine," says Doug Shafer of Shafer Vineyards. "Hillside Select is a special place; it's planted with one hundred percent Cabernet Sauvignon, but it could be Mer-

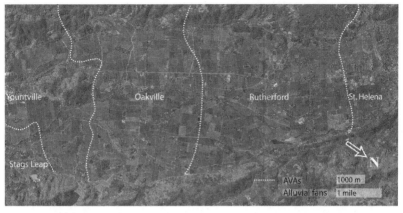

A series of alluvial fans occupies the west side of the valley and also part of the east side.

lot or Cabernet Franc and the special quality of the fruit would still come through." Doug feels that hillsides make better wine than flat lands, but that the gap has narrowed. "Originally we didn't have the tools to make wines from the valley floor. Changes in viticulture mean now you can make wine from the valley floor that is nearly as good as the hillside. You have to work harder; we used denser planting and canopy management to reduce yields. This was not possible ten years ago."

The Napa AVA and sub-AVAs

Well before any regulations were introduced, Napa Valley became an imprimatur of quality on the label. Following the precedent of the French system of appellation contrôlée, the AVA (American Viticultural Area) system was introduced in 1976. This defines a pyramid of wine-producing regions. A broad Napa Valley AVA covers the whole region: as the result of a highly political process, the boundaries go well beyond the valley itself and were drawn to include all vineyards regarding themselves as producing Napa Valley grapes. Covering a total area of 90,000 ha, which represents about half of Napa County, the AVA has about 18,500 ha of vineyards. Given the variation between the south and north, and

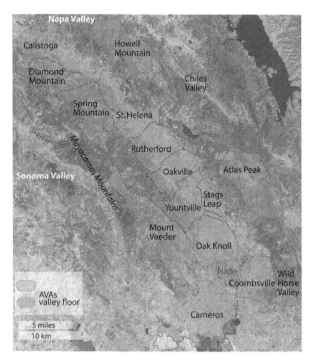

Labels on map:
Napa Valley
Calistoga
Howell Mountain
Diamond Mountain
Chiles Valley
Spring Mountain
St. Helena
Mayacamas Mountains
Rutherford
Sonoma Valley
Oakville
Atlas Peak
Stags Leap
Yountville
Mount Veeder
Oak Knoll
Napa
Wild Horse Valley
Coombsville
AVAs
valley floor
5 miles
10 km
Carneros

Napa Valley has several smaller AVAs within it. (Carneros connects Napa and Sonoma valleys.)

between the valley floor and the mountains, this implies a certain lack of coherence.

AVAs are defined at the instigation of producers in a region, and there are presently fifteen smaller AVAs within the all-encompassing Napa Valley designation. They extend from appellations defining the central valley to mountainous slopes on either side. (Producers often use the term appellation rather than AVA, and will talk about their appellation or sub-appellation wines.) The sub-AVAs tend to have more integrity, and often indicate higher quality wines. About 40% of the vineyards are in the old areas, stretching from Yountville through St. Helena, at the heart of the valley.

Are there really discernable differences between AVAs in the valley? The answer is yes and no. There may be a core to each sub-AVA, but unfortunately the same sorts of political considerations came into play when defining the sub-AVAs that had much reduced the coherence of Napa Valley. The original proposal for the Stags Leap District, for example, expanded to the west, south, and north as producers on the edges clamored to be let in.

The boundaries of the AVAs don't always make it easy to tell whether a particular wine has come from a valley or mountain. The AVAs in the valley often extend up the slopes of the mountains on either side. Pritchard Hill is well known for mountain Cabernets from the vineyards of Bryant, Chappellet, and Colgin, at elevations ranging from 120-330 m—but is included as part of the St. Helena AVA!

The best case for integrity is made by the most famous appellations of the valley proper. The supposed characteristic of Rutherford is a dusty note in the wines. Whether Rutherford Dust is real or is a marketing ploy has long been debated. "The tannins of wines from Rutherford give the sensation you get by running your hand backwards along velvet," was an imaginative description by one producer. I do find a similar quality to the tannins in the wines of several producers. I would not describe it as dusty, more as a sort of slightly sharp tang to the tannins on the finish, but it does give a distinctive tannic grip. But there are other producers whose wines typically have more massive or tighter tannins. I would be prepared to concede a commonality in which firm tannins give the wines a quality I might be inclined to call Rutherford Grip.

In Oakville, the more common pattern in my tastings has been a quality of taut black fruits supported by fine-grained tannins that reinforce an impression of elegance, compared with the greater power of Rutherford. "Oakville is about expressing big berry fruits, a rich character with black olives, and more open tannins," says Mark de Vere of Mondavi. Some wines display a much softer style, with more overt, opulent black fruit aromatics extending from blackcurrants to cassis, and you might argue that they have deserted the communal specificity by going for more approachability in their vinification.

"Cabernets in Stags Leap tend to have richer fruit, with a softer texture," says Doug Shafer, was instrumental in establishing the AVA. Shafer's Hillside Select, one of the top wines of the AVA, which comes from the vineyard rising up behind the winery, epitomizes this quality, with a style of opulent fruits showing evident aromatics. Doug supports his case by recollecting that when Shafer

Bryant Vineyards is the Pritchard Hill area at an elevation of 130 m overlooking Lake Hennessey. It is within the St. Helena AVA.

showed its first 100% Cabernet Sauvignon, it was so approachable that people refused to believe it had no Merlot. But in Stags Leap District generally, I get less impression of consistency today, with many wines that are forward and approachable, showing soft black fruits on the palate, supported by nuts and vanillin on the finish, and tannins noticeable only as a soft, furry presence in the background. These are nice enough for something to drink immediately, but I wonder how it represents Cabernet typicity to make wines that are so fruit-forward and lacking in tannic structure. Again it's a producer's choice, but it seems more common in Stags Leap.

There may be a typicity that distinguishes each AVA if you let it express itself. In any of these appellations, however, you can make soft, forward, fruity, wines with lots of nutty vanillin, using appropriate winemaking techniques to bump up the appeal. Let's at least say that unless you know the producers' styles, the name of the AVA has little predictive value.

The area of the Napa Valley AVA extends far beyond the obvious tourist trails. Well off to the east are Howell Mountain, Chiles Valley, and Atlas Peak. To the west are Diamond Mountain, Spring Mountain, and Mount Veeder. Driving up the twists and turns of the

*The heart of Napa Valley, between Napa and St. Helena, has a monocul-
ture of vineyards, extending across the narrow valley, and confined by the
mountains on either side.*

densely forested roads into the mountains is a completely different
experience from meandering along the center of the valley. Vineyards here are sparsely planted, occupying perhaps 5% of the total
land, contrasted with the monoculture in the valley itself.

The big difference in Napa is really between mountains and
valley: these have different climates and soils. With vineyards often
above the fog line, the climate in the mountains is quite distinct
from the valley itself, where fog is the dominant (and saving) influence. The playoff is that temperatures are reduced by the elevation,
but increased by the lack of fog. There is often more diurnal variation. Mountain vineyards have primary soils with more mineral or
volcanic character, compared with the more alluvial soils deposited
by water flow in the valley. Couple the climatic changes with the
differences in the soils, and you may well ask what connection ex-
ists between the mountain vineyards and those in the valley to
justify both being labeled under the same Napa AVA.

There's a growing tendency to plant Cabernet Sauvignon on
hillsides and mountains rather than on the valley floor, and today
about 14% of the vineyards and 20% of the wineries are on the
mountains (mountain vineyards tend to be smaller). There is quite a
bit of talk in Napa about "mountain tannins." Grapes grown on the
mountains tend to have higher, and sometimes more aggressive,

tannins; getting the tannins ripe at higher altitudes may require a long hang time, with the incidental consequence of later harvests. The grapes protect themselves from the combination of more sunshine (especially higher ultraviolet radiation) and greater wind exposure by increasing their production of anthocyanins and tannins. All this contributes to a tighter structure, especially when the vineyards are above the fog line.

The clearest demonstration of mountain tannins may come from Howell Mountain, on the other side of the valley, where AVA regulations require vineyards to be above the fog line. A tasting of barrel samples from Howell Mountain at David Abreu showed that the interplay of fruit and tannins can practice an unusual deception. At first taste, the wine was surprisingly soft, round, and chocolaty: where were the famous mountain tannins, I wondered? Then 30 seconds later, the finish closed up completely with a massive dose of tannins. That's Howell Mountain for you. "Of all the appellations I would say tannins define Howell Mountain more than any other AVA," says Phillip Corallo-Titus of Chappellet.

Unlike the European system, the statement of an AVA on the label applies only to geographical origin; there is no additional implication of quality, grape variety, or style. When the rules were being discussed in 1979, André Tchelistcheff was sarcastic about the construction of AVAs. "We are not solving the basic elements of appellation, we are not controlling the varietals, we are not controlling the maximum production; I mean we are just trying to fool the consumer that we have appellation of origin."

An AVA label only requires that 85% of the grapes come from the AVA: my view is that this is nowhere near good enough. Considering the premium you pay for Napa Valley, a wine labeled from Napa should have only grapes from Napa. As for vintage, the rules have finally been tightened to specify that wine from an AVA must have 95% of its grapes from the stated vintage. For grape variety, the rule is 75%; this is probably as good as we are going to get, since it started out as 51% when the first federal regulations were introduced in 1936, and was increased (against some opposition) to 75% in 1983. The 75% rule leaves a lot of wiggle room, far too much in my opinion. I would like to see all the rules replaced with a 95% lower limit! (This is what I have set as the standard for describing a wine as "varietal" in the guide to estates.)

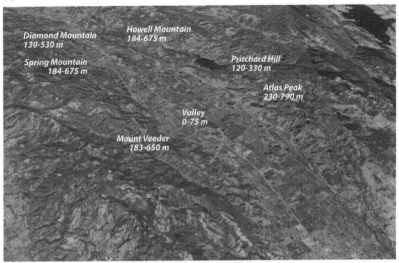

Diamond Mountain
130-530 m

Howell Mountain
184-675 m

Spring Mountain
184-675 m

Pritchard Hill
120-330 m

Atlas Peak
230-790 m

Valley
0-75 m

Mount Veeder
183-650 m

Vineyards in the mountains have significant elevation above those in the valley itself, and conditions are quite different.

A Lack of Old Vines

Napa's character as a young wine region was prolonged by the need to replant many of the vineyards in the nineties. One of the glories of old vineyards is the extra concentration produced in the wine as the vines age. There's no exact measure for what the French would call Vieilles Vignes, but after about twenty years, the yields drop. Perhaps because the lower yields are achieved naturally, the extra concentration seems to have a focus and intensity that is not produced by simply reducing yields by extreme pruning. You might expect the vineyards that were planted during the boom of the 1970s now to have venerable old vines. Unfortunately, a problem with phylloxera put paid to that.

Because of its European origins, Vitis vinifera has no resistance to phylloxera; it must be grafted on to resistant rootstocks from American species of Vitis. Early plantings in Napa used the St. George rootstock, a cultivar of Vitis riparia, which is highly resistant to phylloxera. Its disadvantage is that it can lead the vine to be too

Because the focus on Cabernet Sauvignon is recent, there are not many old vines in Napa Valley. These fifty-year-old vines in the Kronos vineyard are among the oldest.

productive. New plantings during the 1960s and 1970s tended to use AxR1, a rootstock recommended by the Enology Department at the University of California, Davis for its reliability. AxR1 is a hybrid between Vitis vinifera and Vitis rupestris; like many hybrids with some vinifera parentage, it is not really very resistant to phylloxera. The university should have known better, because by the late 1980s, quite predictably, phylloxera was enthusiastically feeding on these rootstocks; unfortunately, by then about 75% of plantings in Napa and Sonoma were on AxR1.

The need to replant vineyards in the 1990s was not entirely a bad thing. "As growers were forced to replant by phylloxera, a lot of the unspoken issues—rootstocks, clones, spacing—became issues for discussion," says Anthony Bell, who had been horrified to find when he came to Beaulieu in 1979 from South Africa that Napa had made itself so vulnerable by planting on a single rootstock. "This was something all Europeans had been told you didn't do," he says.

The only old vines in Napa today are those planted on St. George before the phylloxera epidemic. Sometimes this was the result of calculation, sometimes it was luck, and sometimes *force majeure*. When Al Brounstein created Diamond Creek Vineyards in

1968, he was under pressure to plant AxR1, but he stuck to St George because it had a good record in the mountains. When Cathy Corison purchased her vineyard in Rutherford in the 1990s, the price was reduced because it was thought to be on AxR1—but in fact turned out to be on St. George, and at over forty years old, the vines today are some of the oldest in the valley. When Chateau Montelena planted vineyards in 1974, they tried to do the conventional thing and use AxR1, but it was in so much demand they couldn't get any, so they used St. George. "We were lucky rather than smart," Bo Barrett recalls happily. A side effect of the replacement of AxR1 since the nineties has been an increase in ripeness; the new rootstocks encourage lower yields and more rapid ripening.

Replanting as the result of the AxR1 debacle forced attention on the selection of the cultivar as well. Clones attract more attention in Napa Valley than perhaps anywhere else that focuses on Cabernet Sauvignon. Until the early nineties, there was little choice, but then the French ENTAV clones from Bordeaux became available as well as the old clones that had been propagated from vines previously grown in California. The question about the move towards the ENTAV clones is whether material that was selected in a relatively cool period in Bordeaux will necessarily give the best results in Napa's warmer and drier climate. The most concern is about clone 337, which might compensate for lack of ripeness in Bordeaux, but which really emphasizes lush fruits and supple tannins in the context of Napa.

The Rise of Cult Wines

The nature of the high end has changed somewhat since Napa started concentrating on Cabernet. In 1974, many of the top wines were "Reserves," coming from Beaulieu, Mondavi, or Louis Martini. That has changed. "Reserve really didn't mean much, although the term was popular at the time. Benziger destroyed the use of the term by making a bulk wine. I always resented that. It was quite different from Estate but even that has been diluted now. Today I am amazed that some of the big producers have Estate wines with the California appellation, which to me is ridiculous," says Richard Arrowood,

Many small producers share a tasting room at the Napa Wine Company in Oakville, indicated by the sign to Cult Wine Central

one of the first winemakers to focus on single vineyard wines (in Sonoma).

Today the top wines tend to come from single vineyards, often enough carrying the name of the sub-AVA in which they are located. (However, worried about possible dilution of identity, Napa Valley vintners sponsored a law in 1990 that all wines attributed to any AVA within Napa should in addition mention Napa Valley.) Is the switch in emphasis from reserve bottlings to single vineyards a mark of a maturing wine region? Does this bring Napa more into line with Bordeaux? Well, it remains true that in both cases, the main selling point is the brand, whether or not that brand is associated with geography. But you could make a case that some of the top wines in Napa are more clearly associated with specific terroirs than they are in Bordeaux.

Although there is a definite move towards single vineyards, there are still some leading wines based on barrel selections. It may be true that single vineyards become more interesting at very small production levels, but blending produces more complexity at higher levels. "Separate vineyard wines from the mountains and valley would be like putting handcuffs on us. Not all lots turn out great every year and quality bounces around the valley like a ball. There's wide variation in sources from year to year. In a cool year, St Helena and Calistoga make the best lots, in a warm year it's Napa and the hillsides," says Chuck Wagner, explaining that Caymus Special Selection is usually a blend of one quarter from mountain sources and three quarters from the valley.

Superficially, Napa Valley offers a similar range of wines as Bordeaux, from introductory offerings under $10 per bottle to cults or icons above $100 per bottle. At lower price levels it has something of the same problem as Bordeaux: high costs in Napa make it difficult to compete with varietal Cabernets from the southern hemisphere with lower costs. Moving up market, the recession in 2008 took a toll, with some significant price cuts forced on wines at the top end. Prompted partly by the wish to maintain quality (and exclusivity), and partly by difficulties with the economy, the trend to offer second wines has accentuated in Napa. They have a variety of origins: for cult wines produced in small quantities, they usually come from declassified lots; at larger producers they may represent different sources of material.

Vintage variation is the inevitable companion to expression of terroir. Napa has come a long way from the era when the Wine Institute (an advocacy group representing producers) used the slogan, "Every year is a vintage year in California." That was behind the belief that persisted through the seventies that wine is made by winemaking. Site location and vineyard management were all but dismissed as relevant factors, and it was assumed that California's climate ensured perfect ripeness every year. "The predominant thinking at the time was that every variety would give good results if planted in a good place," Bill Phelps recalls. Matching terroir to varieties and taking account of climatic variation came later. Today at top producers there is more concern to represent the terroir, and recognition that each vintage is different. Indeed, there's a certain disdain at the top Napa producers for technological advice from graduates of the Enology Department of the University of California, Davis. "Graduates from Davis know how to take care of chemicals and things," Fred Schrader says somewhat dismissively. Recollecting Napa's revival, Paul Roberts of Harlan Estate says, "There was the era of students from Davis who came here and said: 'That's how we make wine—going after the correct numbers.' This lasted into the eighties. Today there is more purity and less intervention; we measure numbers but we don't let it drive winemaking." That's the artisanal view.

Famous Vineyards

Some of the top sites in Napa Valley have long histories, with potential that was recognized more than a century ago. At the heart of the Oakville area is the To Kalon vineyard, a parcel of almost 100 ha originally purchased by Hamilton Crabb in 1868 (the name is Greek for "most beautiful"). Further purchases brought Crabb's total to more than 150 ha. Half of the land was planted with hundreds of grape varieties within a few years. Wine was produced under the name of To Kalon vineyards; the best known was "Crabb's Black Burgundy," which actually was made from the Italian Refosco grape. But Cabernet Sauvignon was also grown there in the 1880s.

After various vicissitudes, including changes of ownership, Prohibition, and destruction of the original winery, the vineyard fell into various hands. The major part of more than 100 ha became eventually ended up with Robert Mondavi, whose new winery was positioned at the edge of the original To Kalon vineyard. A minor part of the original To Kalon estate was purchased by Beaulieu Vineyards in 1940, and became the heart of Beaulieu's Private Reserve, but was sold to Andy Beckstoffer in 1993. Beckstoffer sells grapes to a variety of producers, and some of Napa Valley's most expensive Cabernets come from this parcel. It's a measure of the reputation of the vineyard that its grapes from the best known parts sell for close to ten times the average price for Napa Valley Cabernet Sauvignon. The last, smallest part of the original To Kalon vineyard is a parcel of 8 ha that Crabb himself donated to the University of California; this now forms their Oakville Experimental Station. (Probably the most expensive terroir for an experimental station anywhere in the world!)

The To Kalon vineyard occupies the top half of the Oakville Bench—the apex of the fan is more or less at the top of the vine-

Looking down the To Kalon vineyard from the apex of the alluvial fan, there's a slight gradient down to route 29. The scrubby hills beyond the Silverado trail are in the background.

yard. The terroir is a gravelly loam, forming a gradual slope (only just noticeable to the eye) from an elevation of about 75m at the base of the mountains to 50m at the highway. Of course, To Kalon is large for a high quality vineyard, roughly three times the size of the average Grand Cru Classé of the Médoc, so it has significant variation. "Up by the hills it's grand cru terroir, and the wine goes into the Reserve, towards the middle it's premier cru level, and the wine goes into the Oakville Cabernet, down by route 29 it's village territory and the wine goes into a Napa bottling," says Mark de Vere, expressing Mondavi's view.

Just above the To Kalon vineyard is Heitz's famous Martha's vineyard. The Martha's Vineyard 1974 was the first wine from Napa that fooled me at a blind tasting into thinking it came from Bordeaux. I had to be shown the bottle to be convinced I had made a mistake. This hundred percent Cabernet Sauvignon comes from a 14 ha vineyard on the Oakville Bench, just above the To Kalon vineyard. The vineyard itself is not easy to find; there are no signs or directions—perhaps Heitz don't want it covered in day trippers.

The eucalyptus trees at the edge of Martha's Vineyard may have something to do with its famous minty aroma. The Opus One block of To Kalon is on the far side of the trees.

The vineyard was owned by Tom and Martha May, and after a handshake deal, Joe Heitz started to produce wine from its crop in 1966. It was one of the first single vineyard wines of the modern era. The wine is often said to have a minty taste, and even the Heitz web site mentions the string of eucalyptus trees at the edge of the vineyards close to the base of the mountains, but Joe Heitz is re-puted to have believed that the mintiness actually was a property of the vines (which are claimed to come from a proprietary clone pro-ducing unusually small berries). (But when Opus One acquired a block of the To Kalon vineyard on the other side of the trees, they did not like the minty taste in their wine, and cut down some of the trees.) With some shade from the mountains close by, Martha's Vineyard is a little less sunny than some others; possibly this con-tributes to a slightly cooler climate impression and lower alcohol. "For more than two decades, Heitz Martha's Vineyard was the benchmark by which California Cabernets were judged," said Frank Prial of the New York Times in 2000. More recently it has of course followed the inevitable trend towards greater extraction and higher alcohol, but the wine remains relatively restrained for Napa. 1974 probably remains its greatest vintage.

Just across the road from Mondavi, Opus One was one of the first collaborations between Bordeaux and Napa. When Robert Mondavi and Baron Philippe de Rothschild announced the venture, it was seen as a validation of Napa as a winemaking region. Opus One is a Bordeaux Blend strongly (around 85%) dominated by Cabernet Sauvignon. There is probably no clearer example of the French influence on Napa than Dominus winery, located on the old Napanook vineyard, which was one of the first vineyards in Napa Valley, planted on the Oakville alluvial fan by George Yount in 1838. The vineyard was bought by John Daniel, owner of Inglenook, in 1943, and he kept it when he sold Inglenook in 1970. Dominus was first produced as a partnership between Christian Moueix of Château Pétrus in Pomerol and John Daniel's daughter, and then in 1995 Christian became sole owner. The change in varietal constitution over the years is one sign of the adjustment from Bordeaux to Napa. "When Dominus started we had 21% Merlot; now it's only 0.2%. Cabernet Sauvignon has gone from 65% to 85%. The initial plantings were prejudged from Bordeaux, that you could transpose percentages from Bordeaux to Napa and it would work," says winemaker Tod Mostero.

At the northern end of the valley, just to the east of Calistoga, the Eisele vineyard is another of Napa's famous sites. It was first planted as a vineyard in 1886; this was around twenty to thirty years after much of the valley was planted to wheat, but the soils here were too poor, and probably vines were the first crop to be planted. There was a variety of cépages, originally Zinfandel and Riesling, but nothing very distinguished until Cabernet Sauvignon was planted in 1964, when it was field grafted on to the old roots. The Eisele's sold the grapes, and "Phelps Eisele 1975 was the benchmark wine for years and years," Fred Schrader said, when I asked him what was the first Napa cult wine. Phelps continued to produce its Eisele Cabernet until Bart and Daphne Araujo purchased the vineyard in 1990.

Mountain Vineyards

Eisele has an unusual terroir. The vineyards are on an alluvial fan coming straight off the Palisades mountains, but they are not very fertile, and fertility *decreases* going away from the mountain. Going up the slope you get more clay soils and higher vigor, the opposite of the usual order. Pebbles washed down from the Palisades to make a thick layer of subsoil about one foot deep all over the western block of the vineyard, which is effectively bisected by Simmons Creek. The creek—dry most of the time, but prone to fill up and even flash flood—is full of round pebbles. This is the most gravelly part of the vineyard, and in true Bordeaux style, it is planted entirely with Cabernet Sauvignon. The blocks on the eastern side are planted with a variety of cépages, mostly Merlot and Syrah for the blacks, and at the farthest east, some white varieties.

When Hamilton Crabb planted the To Kalon vineyard, it was just a matter of clearing the land and digging in the grapevines. Switching the use of the land to viticulture, especially as it becomes

Eisele vineyard is in Simmons Creek Canyon, a protected area to the east of the Silverado trail (parallel to the bottom of the image). Elevation rises from 111 m at the lowest point to 134 m at the edge of the mountain. Simmons Creek (dry most of the year) runs through the vineyard.

a monoculture, creates a certain change in the environment, but the terroir remains recognizably the same. This has not necessarily remained true as vineyard plantings have extended to mountains. When the first vineyards were carved out of mountain sites around Napa in the 1960s and 1970s, no one thought much of it (aside from questioning whether the sites were appropriate for the intended varieties). By the 1980s, people began to object to terraforming. One trigger was the construction of Atlas Peak Vineyards. As described by the project manager, Dick Peterson, "There are D10 Cats up there. This is a moonscape, but we're ripping it. We'll put terraces in there...We'll fill that canyon with rocks the size of Volkswagens, then cover it up with some muck from the caves we're digging."

Mountain reconstructions became controversial. When Delia Viader constructed her vineyard on Howell Mountain, environmental damage to Bell Canyon Reservoir below led to civil law suits and criminal charges. Today the growth of mountain vineyards has slowed dramatically. Given the much higher costs associated with creating and maintaining mountain vineyards, it's not surprising that they should include a concentration of high-end wineries; indeed, many of Napa's cult wines come from mountain sites.

Perhaps at the end of the day (environmental issues aside) the question is not whether a terroir is natural or artificial, but whether it is good for growing grapes. Or in the context of Cabernet Sauvignon, what's the difference in making wine from grapes grown on a mountain as opposed to in the valley? Indeed, it's curious that attempts in Napa to produce wines like Bordeaux should focus on mountain vineyards. Bordeaux, after all, is pretty flat, and the principal distinction between sites is whether they are gravel-based or clay-based. But Bill Harlan at Harlan Estate (on the mountain above Oakville) and Al Brounstein at Diamond Creek Vineyards (on Diamond Mountain) felt that vineyards in the valley would not give the small berries that they needed for the highest quality Cabernet Sauvignon. "I wanted to create a first growth in California. All at once I started looking for a totally different type of land that would produce the best fruit, not necessarily look nice. Historically the best wine produced in America over a long period of time was the Rutherford Bench, but after studying soils I became convinced we wanted to be on the hillside with good drainage," says Bill Harlan.

Harlan Estate, which made one of the first "cult" wines in Napa, is on the mountain slopes at Oakville, looking out over Martha's Vineyard, To Kalon, and Napanook, lower in the valley.

"Al felt that grapes from hillsides suffer more, and would give more intensity," Phil Ross at Diamond Creek recalls.

The Style of Napa

"Napa Valley is more a concept than a sense of place—it has become a brand and a style in itself," one producer said to me. "Napa Cabernet is the only New World wine ruler that's being used internationally—it wins price, volume, and scores. The reason it's the market winner is because the word *Napa* is a brand," says Leo McCloskey, of Enologix, a company that advises producers on how to increase the impact of their wines in the marketplace. The question about Napa is to what extent there is uniformity of style, and how important are climate and land as opposed to winemaking? It's probably fair to say that winemaking with Cabernet Sauvignon is less variable than with some other varieties. The most significant factor affecting style is the choice of when to harvest, and certainly the trend towards achieving greater ripeness by later harvesting has played to Napa's general strengths: lots of sunshine and not much water. Insofar as there is a common style, it's an emphasis on ripe fruits that is encouraged by the climate.

Sonoma Valley

"Napa is all about Cabernet Sauvignon and Bordeaux varieties, Sonoma is a jigsaw of varieties and is about diversity," says Mark Lingenfelder of Chalk Hill Winery. Sonoma County is about twice the area of Napa County, but has a comparable area of vineyards: reflecting their relative positions in the hierarchy of California wine regions, the crop is somewhat larger, but its value is somewhat less. Napa's intense concentration on Cabernet Sauvignon for reds and Chardonnay for whites has led to its being viewed as the leader for both, but in fact Sonoma produces three times as much Chardonnay as Napa and almost as much Cabernet Sauvignon. Cabernet is the most important black variety grown in Sonoma, but Sonoma is more diverse, since it produces almost as much Pinot Noir. "In Napa, Cabernet is king, but in Sonoma it's more one of a variety of grapes," says winemaker Margo Van Staaveren at Chateau St. Jean.

The feeling in Sonoma is quite different from Napa. As you drive up to Sonoma from San Francisco, the valley is much less confined than Napa Valley. The Coastal Range Mountains are well off to the west between Sonoma and the Pacific, and the Mayacamas Mountains are away to the east. Driving right through Sonoma, route 101 is a highway with the usual depressing industrial developments on either side once you enter the valley above Petaluma. This is quite a contrast with the chic wineries and tasting rooms along route 29 in Napa. However, when you get off the beaten track, there are numerous winding roads running through hillside slopes patterned with vineyards; wineries are indicated rather discretely. Several of the valleys come together at Healdsburg, a gentrified town just off the freeway. The average scale of production in Sonoma is smaller; vineyards are divided among 1,800 growers, compared with 600 vineyard owners in Napa.

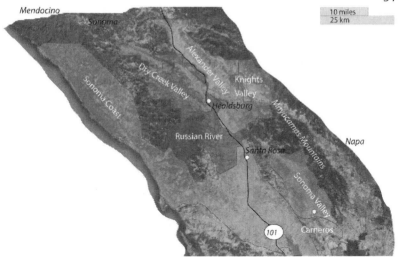

Sonoma County has 15 AVAs (some contained within others). Only the major areas are shown here.

Sonoma County is a relatively large area, extending from the coast to the Mayacamas Mountains separating it from Napa County. Labeled Sonoma County, a wine can come from anywhere in the area. Only a minor step up, Sonoma Coast is a vast coastal area without particularly distinguished terroir, although within it are some individual vineyards with good reputations. Coming to the regions of highest quality, it might be more appropriate to talk about Sonoma Valleys in the plural, since in addition to the eponymous Sonoma Valley itself, there are several other valleys, each with its own characteristics. The AVA of Sonoma Valley is to the north of the town of Sonoma, centered on the Sonoma river. The other areas of interest are the valleys formed by rivers that drain into the Sonoma river (a contrast with Napa Valley, where the areas of interest are the mountain slopes on either side of the valley bottom). The best known valleys in Sonoma are the Russian River Valley (for Pinot Noir), Alexander Valley (for Cabernet Sauvignon), and Dry Creek Valley (for Zinfandel).

Closer to the breezes and fogs from the Pacific, Sonoma is on average cooler than Napa, with growing season temperatures in Santa Rosa, on the edge of the Russian River Valley, up to a degree

Mendocino

Sonoma

Alexander Valley

Dry Creek Valley

Knights Valley

Healdsburg

Russian River

Santa Rosa

Mayacamas Mountains

Sonoma Valley

Carneros

101

10 miles
25 km

zone 3
zone 2
zone 1

The climate becomes steadily warmer moving inland. Alexander Valley and Dry Creek Valley are variable, but are the warmest sites, together with parts of Sonoma Valley.

less than Napa. This is why Pinot Noir can succeed in Sonoma while it is rarely successful in Napa. By the same measure, Cabernet Sauvignon might be expected to show more of a cool climate character. Microclimates are if anything more important in Sonoma than Napa, with wide variation in soils and temperatures. There's more Cabernet Sauvignon in the warmer valleys, Alexander, Dry Creek, and Sonoma, and very little in Russian River, which has a sharp focus on Pinot Noir.

Although there's a great diversity of soil types in Sonoma, possibly it's more to the point that terrains vary from valley floor, to rolling hills, to mountainous. Russian River Valley is the most consistent, with some vineyards on the flat land along the river, and the rest on low, gentle slopes. The most dramatic contrasts are to be found in Alexander and Sonoma Valleys, which vary from vineyards on relatively fertile flat soil in the center to vertiginous slopes up to several hundred meters of elevation on the mountains.

Dry Creek and Alexander Valleys run parallel to the north of Healdsburg. Closer to the coast, Dry Creek is a broad valley, cool at the southern end and warm at the northern end, growing a wide range of varietals from Pinot Noir at the south, to Cabernet in the middle, and Zinfandel in the north. It's by far best known for its Zinfandels, and indeed perhaps this is the one region in California where Zinfandel can be taken seriously as a grape that reflects terroir and produces ageworthy wines.

With that perverse reversal of the usual north-south, cool to warm, relationship, Alexander Valley, the most northern AVA of Sonoma, is where Cabernet Sauvignon does best. The Cabernets lack that extreme lushness found in Napa Valley and can offer a more restrained impression, as indeed also can the Zinfandels, especially those from around Geyserville, which rival those of Dry Creek Valley.

Pinot Noir in Russian River Valley

Pinot Noir has had a chequered history in California. Attempts to grow it for varietal production during the initial burst of enthusiasm for European varieties in the late nineteenth century were largely unsuccessful. In fact, wines labeled as "Burgundy" were as likely to be made from Zinfandel as from Pinot Noir. After the debacle of Prohibition, Pinot Noir was pioneered by Louis Martini in Carneros, but never achieved any penetration comparable to Cabernet Sauvignon, which soon emerged as the quality black variety of choice. Part of the problem was the failure to define appropriate viticultural conditions for Pinot Noir, which was often planted next to Cabernet Sauvignon in sites that were simply too warm for it. And vinification was not adjusted for the variety. Josh Jensen (who founded the Calera Wine Company) comments that "most wineries had a standard red wine method" that was applied indiscriminately.

Attempts to produce quality Pinot Noir started in the 1970s, some of the pivotal moments being in 1973 when Joe Swan released his first Pinot Noir from Russian River, and Davis Bynum produced the first single vineyard Pinot Noir (from the Rochioli vineyard). More idiosyncratic in his choice of location, Josh Jensen planted the first vineyards for Calera Wine on Mount Harlan in 1975. But during the seventies and eighties, many wineries gave up attempts to produce Pinot Noir as part of a general belief that Pinot Noir belonged in Burgundy, not California. Looking back, Rod Ber

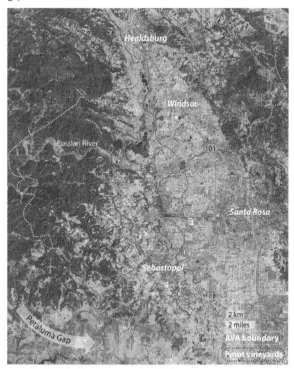

The Russian River AVA extends south of Healdsburg. Most of the Pinot Noir vineyards lie between Healdsburg and Sebastopol.

glund of Joseph Swan Vineyards comments that, "The oldest vines in the estate were planted in 1969. Anyone who planted Pinot Noir at that time was a visionary or a lunatic, and to say they were a visionary is revisionist history."

Pinot Noir is grown all over Sonoma, and bottlings range from Sonoma Coast AVA, meaning anywhere in the vast area, to single vineyard names. Because of geological history, there is a great variety of soil types; in fact, they are fond of saying locally that there are more soil types in Sonoma Valley than in the whole of France. The best known area is the Russian River Valley, one of several valleys that come together at the town of Healdsburg. The Russian River used to flow directly south to San Pablo Bay, but volcanic eruptions some millions of years ago caused it to swing west to where it now empties out into the Pacific.

Russian River has gently rolling hills.

Russian River Valley, running to the south of Healdsburg, is Pinot Noir Central. The style is richer than Burgundy. "We don't make Burgundy and don't try to. We make Russian River Pinot Noir, " says Bob Cabral, winemaker of Williams-Selyem, whose single-vineyard Pinots sell exclusively to a mailing list that isn't easy to join. "Russian River Pinots are deeply textured wines with dark fruits," he says, adding that "we make really ripe wines but we try not to get too ripe." There is also, of course, a good amount of Chardonnay produced in Russian River.

The terrain in Russian River Valley varies from flat expanses near the river to gently rolling hills. Soils vary, alluvial in the flood plain immediately around the river, sandstone, granite, or sandy loam elsewhere. There is more homogeneity to the west of Sebastopol, where soils are based on the so-called Goldridge loam. Just to the south of the Russian River Valley is the Petaluma gap, where a break in the mountains allows cool air to sweep from the Pacific across to San Francisco Bay, providing lots of fog and an important cooling influence. Penetration by coastal fog is the important climatic influence; indeed, there have been attempts to redefine the boundaries of the AVA to confine it to the area covered by the fogs. Resulting from proximity to the ocean, the western side of the AVA is cooler than the eastern. Overall the coolest part of the valley is the sub-AVA of Green Valley at the southern end. Today there are more than 6,000 ha of vineyards in Russian River Valley, with Chardonnay as the lead variety, followed by Pinot Noir; together they are close to three quarters of all plantings. Some top vineyards lie to the west of Russian River in the area known to locals as "True Sonoma Coast," to distinguish it from the broad AVA. It is fair to say these are not delicate wines; the style fairly bursts with fruit.

If I had to use just a single word to describe the Pinot Noir of Russian River, it would be "sumptuous." The fruits are almost always forward, the impression on the palate is rich, tannins are rarely obvious. But vineyard differences come through the rich style. Russian River may have as many individual vineyard designations for its Pinot Noirs as anywhere on the West Coast. The highly varied soil types make any general grouping rather difficult. Together with variations in exposure to fog and general aspect of the land, not to mention clones and the age of the vines, the individual site acquires increased importance. If you ask winegrowers to disentangle which of these influences are the more important, they shrug and say, "all of the above." But although winegrowers are certainly sensitive to variations in the quality and style of wines that come from different vineyard sources, you rarely hear anyone try to relate that quality or style to the specifics of the soil type as they might in Burgundy. You get the impression that climate is at least a more identifiable factor. Indeed, the most important single factor may be the hours of fog, which determine the daily growing temperature. Take the difference between the Hirsch Vineyard in Sonoma Coast and the Rochioli River Block vineyard in Russian River, for example.

The Hirsch vineyard is 13 miles northwest of River Block as the crow flies. Average elevation is around 450 m, and the top part of the vineyard is above the fog line. Grapes develop thicker skins and therefore more tannins here. It flowers and harvests about one month later each year, and shows more variation with vintage, compared to River Block. River Block is on sandier soils in the Russian River flood plain. The major characteristic of the wine is its finesse. A comparison of Williams Selyem's single vineyard wines

The Middle Reach of Russian River running along Westside Road is a flat flood plain. Russian River is behind the trees and last flooded these vineyards in 1995.

over two decades showed that the same thread of commonality runs through each vineyard as it shows its character over a series of vintages. Hirsch is deeper and broader, River Block is tighter and lighter. You might say that Hirsch is more masculine and River Block is more feminine. In each year, River Block is more developed and I perceive a touch more complexity. The reflections of these nuances through vintage are every bit as interesting as a comparison of two premier crus in Burgundy.

Cabernet Sauvignon in Sonoma

My recollection of styles from the first Cabernet Sauvignons I tasted from Sonoma in the seventies is that they were distinctly leaner than Napa, not so surprising given Sonoma's slightly cooler climate. (Those wines would have come from valley floor sites that today would probably not be regarded as optimal for Cabernet.) That leaner quality does not seem to be true today; certainly as judged by alcohol levels, the Cabernets of Sonoma are right up there with Napa. "Sonoma even to a greater degree than Napa has more vagaries in climate and terroir. It probably was true that Sonoma Cabernet was leaner than Napa in the seventies but not so much now. There is more knowledge now about where to plant Cabernet, we know it needs to be in the warmer sites on hillsides, it used to be on the valley floor," says winemaker Richard Arrowood, who was there right at the beginning, producing Cabernet Sauvignon first at Chateau St. Jean later at Arrowood, and now at his latest venture, Amapola Creek. Part of the reason the difference has apparently lessened may be the increased concentration on growing Cabernet in mountain vineyards, which may be more similar between Sonoma and Napa than are the valley floors.

Perhaps because of that initial leanness, there seems to have been more concern to soften the Cabernet with other varieties in Sonoma. "Green bean character in Cabernet Sauvignon was typical in the 1990s. Then Parker came along and it became unacceptable," says Rob Davis, who has been making wine at Jordan Vineyards since the seventies. "The wines made in the seventies were fairly extracted; there wasn't this 'I want to take it home and drink it tonight'—you really had to lay them down. We thought that blending would make a softer wine," says Margo Van Staaveren, who has been at Chateau St. Jean throughout. This was the impetus for Chateau St. Jean's introduction of Cinq Cepages in 1990, a wine made from all five classic Bordeaux varieties. "The idea was to have approachability, accessibility, and ageability; they weren't accessible wines we made in the seventies," she recollects. "I have Napa envy, they get the lush rich textures that are not so easy to come by in Sonoma," she adds.

Opinions have oscillated on blends versus varietals. "The early vineyard designates were all 100% Cabernet Sauvignon. There weren't a lot of the other varieties—when there was a blend the cheapest variety was the Cabernet Sauvignon!—you couldn't find the other varieties," Richard Arrowood recollects about the early days at Chateau St. Jean. Things went in the other direction at Arrowood, where Richard made the wines through the nineties. The two top wines were the monovarietal Cabernet Sauvignon from the Monte Rosso vineyard and the Réserve Spéciale, a blend from several vineyards. The reserve has undergone an interesting transition.

The Monte Rosso vineyard occupies a peak at 375 m in the Mayacamas Mountains with direct exposure to San Pablo Bay, fifteen miles away. Courtesy Louis Martini.

"With the reserve at the beginning we started with a blend, but we wanted to get more structure," says current winemaker Heidi von der Mehden. The Reserve was a classic blend of four Bordeaux varieties until 1993, but then changed to a 100% Cabernet Sauvignon. I think this may have been a mistake; comparing the 1997 monovarietal with the 1993 blend, there seems to be a certain something missing. I'm inclined to the view that it is only an exceptional site in Sonoma that will make a really successful monovarietal Cabernet. The exception that proves the rule is the Monte Rosso Vineyard.

Probably the most famous vineyard in Sonoma, the Monte Rosso ranch has 100 ha of vines spread out over 250 ha at the peak of the mountain with views across to San Pablo Bay. As the name suggests, it has rocky, red volcanic soils; most of the topsoils are 18-24 inches deep, based on pure rock. Exposure to the bay ensures cool breezes all day and keeps up the acidity in the berries. It was originally planted by Emanuel Goldstein in the early 1880s with a

The rusty red appearance of the iron-rich soils lives up to Monte Rosso's name.

wide mix of varieties. The vineyard was wiped out by phylloxera and replanted in 1890, when Zinfandel became a significant part of the plantings. Some of these old vines still remain as blocks of Zinfandel or field blends with Alicante and Beaunoir. When Louis Martini took over the vineyard in 1938, they concentrated on Zinfandel and Cabernet Sauvignon. (In the interim, they called the wine Monte Rosso Chianti.) Among the plantings from 1938, the surviving Cabernet Sauvignon vines are probably the oldest Cabernet in the USA.

Following the sale of Louis Martini, since 2002 the Monte Rosso vineyard has been part of the Gallo Empire. Louis Martini takes the bulk of production, but still sells grapes to other producers. There have been experiments with various blends, but the monovarietal Cabernets from Monte Rosso certainly stand out. What I especially like about Louis Martini's Monte Rosso Cabernet is the precise expression of black fruit without the jammy overtones that often accompany big wines in Napa. Arrowood's Monte Rosso is perhaps a touch more precise, and Sbragia's a little softer. The

Vines planted as individual bushes in 1938 at the Monte Rosso vineyard are probably the oldest Cabernet Sauvignon in the United States.

common thread is a sense of elegance, a fine structure supporting the fruits.

Santa Cruz Mountains

The doyen of Cabernet Sauvignon in California in the modern era might not be in Napa or Sonoma at all, but in the Santa Cruz Mountains just south of San Francisco. Wine production started at Ridge in the nineteenth century, although it lacks the continuous history of Beaulieu or Inglenook, having closed during Prohibition; it was revived in the 1960s. Another couple of peaks along the mountain range, Martin Ray established his winery in the 1940s. After he left in 1970, it became the Mount Eden vineyard. Both Ridge and Mount Eden have a long history with Cabernet Sauvignon. The vines for both properties originated with a selection brought from Margaux in the nineteenth century by Emmet Rixford (no one is sure whether the wines actually came from Château Mar-

From the steep, elevated vineyards in Santa Cruz, there are views over San Francisco Bay fifty miles to the north and west.

gaux or merely from the Margaux appellation). The original plantings are still propagated by selection massale at both wineries.

A cool climate for Cabernet Sauvignon, the Santa Cruz mountain appellation has roughly equal amounts of Pinot Noir, Chardonnay, and Cabernet Sauvignon (and then a mix of other varieties). With vineyards at altitudes from 400 to 800 m, exposed to cooling influences from the Pacific only a few miles away, the style is more moderate than Napa or Sonoma. "Santa Cruz is more soil-driven than fruit-driven and appeals to a more Eurocentric style. Alcohol levels here are usually lower," says winemaker Jeffrey Patterson at Mount Eden. Today the Cabernet Sauvignon is a blend at the varietal limit, usually with 75% Cabernet Sauvignon, and the rest mostly Merlot. Until 2000 there was also a monovarietal Cabernet Sauvignon made from old vines planted by Martin Ray in the 1950s (on their own roots!) They had to be replanted because they had essentially stopped producing. We tasted a very interesting comparison between the blend and the Old Vine Reserve from 1994. The two wines come from the same mountain top, same scion. You see the same relative difference as elsewhere: the monovarietal is more precise, tighter, less developed; the blend has lost that precise delineation of fruits, but has gained some roundness, development, and flavor variety. In terms of the development of old wine, I prefer the blend, although the Old Vine Reserve certainly has something extra from the concentration of the old vines.

The topsoils in the mountains are thin, based on shale. At Ridge, there is an unusual terroir, with a fractured layer of limestone overlaid with green stone (a highly friable sedimentary rock). The vine roots penetrate easily through the green stone and can go into the limestone. Is it the terroir that's responsible for the minerality in the wines or just better retention of acidity due to the cooler climate? The wines are long lived. "The natural instinct of the vineyards here is to make a 25 year wine," says Jeffrey Patterson. And that is certainly true of Ridge, where the Cabernets begin to develop well after a decade and may last for three or more decades. Ridge's Montebello vineyard is one of the most famous in California, and produces one of the longest-lived wines.

The modern history of Ridge began when a group of engineers from Stanford University bought the property on the Santa Cruz Mountains south of San Francisco in 1959 and started producing Cabernet Sauvignon from vines that had been planted in the 1940s. Over the next few years they expanded the vineyard area from 6 to 18 ha (introducing Zinfandel from 1964), and production grew to about 3,000 cases. Paul Draper, a Stanford philosophy graduate who had been making wine in Chile, joined in 1969 because he was so impressed with the 1962 and 1964 Cabernets (both monovarietal). "It was the first time I tasted California wine, outside of the old Inglenook and Beaulieu wines, with the complexity of Bordeaux. Those two wines were the reason why I joined Ridge. The wines were completely natural," he says.

Ridge Vineyards is actually an amalgam of several different vineyards all planted along the Monte Bello Ridge, which runs roughly northwest to south-east. Both terroir and climate are different from Napa and Sonoma on the North Coast. This explains the moderate character of the wines. "We are too cool here to do what Napa is doing and anyway I don't like the style. My reference point was Château Latour, until Bordeaux began to change. We stayed with the style of moderate alcohol. For the first forty years it was 12.9%, now it is around 13.1%," Paul says. Because the vineyards are located literally on a ridge, every parcel has a slightly different exposure and has been planted ac-cordingly with the intention of achieving even ripening. "When I say fully ripe I get into a definition that has become—I shouldn't say controversial—but California has a totally different interpretation of what ripeness is. In the Santa

Vineyards on Santa Cruz mountains look out over Silicon Valley to the east. Courtesy Ridge Vineyards.

Cruz mountains the average temperature is the same as Bordeaux but the nights are cooler and for that reason we retain acidity much better than elsewhere in California, such as Napa. We have never added acidity but sometimes we have had to precipitate it out."

Monte Bello is a blend, and perhaps not surprisingly considering Paul's traditional imperatives, closer to Bordeaux in its varietal composition than to a Napa Cabernet. The transition took a while, from the monovarietal of the early sixties, to a wine with over 90% Cabernet Sauvignon in the eighties, and then to a range over the past two decades from a minimum of 56% to a maximum of 85%. Merlot is always the second most important variety, with smaller amounts of Petit Verdot and Cabernet Franc. Monte Bello is a long-lived wine; Paul thinks it begin to show its characteristics around 9-12 years of age, and develops until it is 20 or 30 years old. As for really old vintages, the 1974 was only just past its peak at 35 years of age, and the 1964 was rather tertiary but still enjoyable at 45 years. I can't help but wonder how much the moderate style of the wines is a key factor in ensuring such longevity.

Limestone in Mount Harlan

In the Santa Cruz Mountains, microclimates vary to the point at which on successive ridges (within five miles as the crow flies), you can find the famous Ridge Montebello vineyard where Cabernet Sauvignon triumphs, and Fogarty's vineyards of Pinot Noir. An hour or so farther south on Mount Harlan are the vineyards where Josh Jensen founded Calera Wines in 1972 when he found limestone.

Soils in Santa Cruz Mountains are shale or sandstone, generally without much clay. Perhaps because the area is circumscribed, Santa Cruz is one of the few AVAs to be relatively unaffected by politics. Vineyards have to be above the fog line. Here the pattern is the reverse of elsewhere with morning sun and afternoon fog. Thomas Fogarty was the pioneer for Pinot Noir, but now has been followed by several others. The wines tend to spicy black fruits with good tannic support, and age well for up to two decades.

"Trespassers will be transmogrificated," says the sign at the entrance to Calera Wine Company on Mount Harlan, an indication that Josh Jensen has lost none of his feisty character with age. As an avowed Burgundian, Josh believes that nothing but limestone terroir can make great Pinot Noir. "For me the definition of great wine is that it's extremely complex. The classic great Pinot Noirs are grown on limestone soils—I took as my theoretical start on Pinot Noir that they were great because they were grown on limestone. All of the vineyards here are on limestone," he told me. That simple statement belies a long and dedicated search for limestone terroir in California.

After spending 1969 and 1970 working in Burgundy, including a spell at Romanée Conti, Josh Jensen returned to the United States with the ambition of growing great Pinot Noir. He looked for limestone terroir all over California, and finally found a marker in the form of an old lime kiln (used to produce lime at a quarry) on Mount Harlan. The name of his company reflects these origins; Calera is the Spanish for lime kiln. At almost 700 m elevation, the vineyards are among the highest (and coolest) in the United States. The cool climate comes not only from the elevation but also from cold breezes and fog direct from the Pacific, only a few miles away.

An old lime kiln gave the clue that this was the terroir for Pinot Noir where Calera was established. Photograph courtesy Calera Wine Company.

The vineyards are well isolated from all other vineyards, the nearest being the Santa Cruz Mountain AVA fifty miles to the north. Calera's unique quality is recognized in the existence of the Mount Harlan AVA in which it is the only winery.

Spread over more than 250 hectares on the mountain, there are now six separate Pinot Noir vineyards. Selleck, Jensen, and Reed were planted in 1975; Mills, Ryan, and De Villiers were planted between 1984 and 2001. (Mills vineyard is on its own roots; the soil may be sandy enough to have some resistance to phylloxera, and the vineyards are isolated.) Most of the plantings are the Calera selection, which came from 18 original vines at Chalone. (No one will comment any more on the old story that the original source of these vines was cuttings liberated from Romanée Conti. It's often described as the Calera clone, but in fact consists of a selection with some variations.) The wines of each vineyard have their own character; there is also a Mount Harlan cuvée that includes lots declassified from the individual vineyards. The two vineyards that give the most different wines are Selleck and Reed, close together but on opposite sides of a stream with opposed aspects. Selleck faces south and makes Calera's most intense wine; Reed faces north and makes the lightest wine.

In the earliest vintages, from 1978-1981, the aim was to have 12.5% alcohol. Then Josh started picking a little later to get greater ripeness, and the wines went to 13.5%. In the past decade there's been some bracket creep, picking a little riper each year, but Josh says that since 2005 there's been a pull back to earlier picking. Usually each vineyard is harvested in several batches, typically producing more sugar (higher potential alcohol) in the later pickings. The assemblage can give more complexity than a single picking. "If you aspire to make great wines, you often have to take risks, you are living on a knife's edge between picking too early and picking too late," says Jensen. In spite of the cool climate and the limestone soils, usually it's necessary to acidify. Jensen's winemaking may be more Burgundian than the Burgundians: there's no protracted cold soak, most grapes go into the vat as uncrushed whole clusters, fermentation occurs naturally by indigenous yeasts, and continues until the cap falls.

Overall it's just a fraction warmer here than in Burgundy, but the key to character and ageability, Josh says, is the soil. Tasting a horizontal of Calera's single vineyard wines is an exercise comparable to travelling from the Côte de Beaune to the Côte de Nuits, with de Villiers, Mills, and Reed on the lighter side with a red fruit spectrum, Ryan offering a half way house, and Jensen and Selleck showing greater density and structure in a black fruit spectrum. There is no mistaking the differences. The wines have savory and even herbaceous elements in the Old World style, but the forwardness of the sweet ripe fruits and the high alcohol is New World. Wines from the lighter vineyards seem to lose some of their distinction with age, however, and reach a peak somewhere under a decade. Jensen and Selleck are the wines with real aging potential. I felt Josh had gone a long way towards proving his point about aging on limestone when I tasted the 1990 Jensen vineyard, whose savory notes and delicious tones of sous bois seemed quite Burgundian. Perhaps it ages just a little more quickly than Burgundy; in a blind tasting, had I placed this as Burgundy, I would have thought about the 1985 vintage.

Vintages

Vintage	Rating	Notes	Average alcohol in Napa Cabernet
2014	92	Precocious Spring, dry summer, and early harvest gave strong wines, but not as intense as 2013.	14.9%
2013	94	Considered an ideal season with dry, sunny conditions; the downside is high alcohol. Wines are intense, rich, and muscular.	15.2%
2012	93	Return to classic conditions with well-structured wines. Many vintners consider this the best vintage since 2007.	14.5%
2011	86	A problem vintage because of cool weather and rain, giving lower alcohol levels and lighter wines; sometimes difficult to get the right balance with ripeness.	13.7%
2010	88	Reduced in size by problems in Spring, with cool conditions followed by heat in late summer. Said to be elegant, but sometimes a bit lacking in character.	14.1%
2009	89	Mild summer, even conditions, wines a bit on lighter side tending to softness for early drinking.	14.5%
2008	90	Reduced in size by Spring frosts, giving concentrated wines that may take time to come around.	14.8%

2007	*94*	Lush, opulent wines in Napa's modern style, well received and universally praised.	*14.7%*
2006	*90*	Slightly lighter vintage that did not attract much attention.	*14.8%*
2005	*92*	Cooler, longer growing season gave structured wines. Questions is whether fruits will outlive tannins in the long run.	*14.5%*
2004	*91*	Early harvest resulted from heat in August. Big, rich wines, maturing relatively early.	*14.9%*
2003	*88*	Irregular conditions with cool growing season followed by hot September, generally for drinking early.	*14.4%*
2002	*92*	Classic in the new Napa style tending to richness and opulence.	*14.6%*
2001	*93*	Even, long growing season gave well-structured wines thought to be long-lived, but I find them a bit lacking in generosity.	*14.3%*
2000	*86*	Summer heat waves followed by October rains gave tight acidic wines that were not very well received.	*13.8%*

Vineyard Profiles

Ratings	
***	*Excellent producers defining the very best of the appellation*
**	*Top producers whose wines typify the appellation*
*	*Very good producers making wines of character that rarely disappoint*

Symbols

Address

Phone

Contact

Email

Link

Viticultural Area

Pure Varietal (>95%)

Blended red wine

Second label

White wine

Sustainable Viticulture

Organic

Biodynamic

Tastings/visits possible

By appointment only

No visits

Cellar Door Sales

No direct sales

acres = estate vineyards; bottles = annual production

Napa

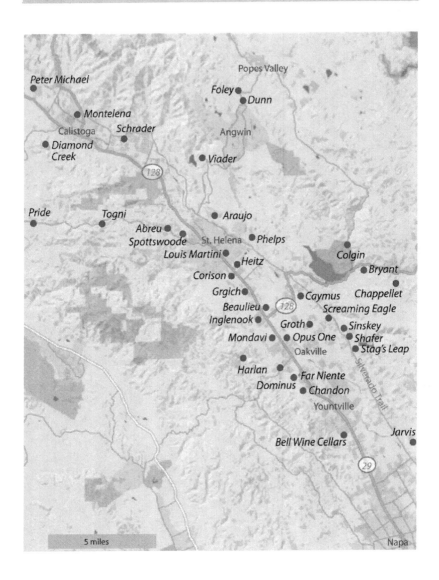

Peter Michael

Popes Valley

Foley
Dunn

Montelena

Calistoga Schrader

Angwin

Diamond
Creek

Viader

128

Pride   Togni

Araujo

Abreu

Spottswoode   St. Helena   Phelps

Louis Martini

Heitz

Colgin

Corison

Bryant

Grgich

Caymus   Chappellet

Beaulieu   128

Screaming Eagle

Inglenook   Groth

Sinskey

Mondavi   Opus One   Shafer

Oakville

Stag's Leap

Harlan

Far Niente

Dominus   Chandon

Yountville

Jarvis

Bell Wine Cellars

29

5 miles

Napa

Silverado Trail

Abreu Vineyards **

2366 Madrona Ave, Saint Helena, CA 94574

(1) 707 963 7487

info@abreuvineyard.com

Brad Grimes

www.abreuvineyards.com

Napa Valley

Napa, Madrona Ranch, Cabernet Sauvignon

69 acres; 12,000 bottles

David Abreu has long been famous as a grape grower, Many producers will tell you proudly that a cuvée comes from one of the Abreu vineyards, and Abreu grapes are behind a fair number of Napa's cult wines. Abreu has four properties, totaling about 70 acres, and he now keeps grapes from 20-25 acres for making his own wine. Each of the vineyards—Madrona, Capella, Thorevilos, and Howell Mountain—has all the Bordeaux varieties. Madrona Ranch is the most famous of the holdings, unusual for its red strip of ferrous soil. There's 65-70% Cabernet Sauvignon at Capella, 45-60% at the others, and some Malbec at Howell Mountain. The facility is a long branching tunnel into the hill, dug in 1979, extended in 1982, then finished in 2006. All the wine is made here in a long row of 2 ton fermenters, There's 100% new oak, 2-3 rackings, no fining: "no reason to fine at all," says winemaker Brad Grimes. Lots are picked when ready and then cofermented irrespective of variety. "One of the advantages of cofermentation is that you can usually balance out acid and alcohol. People tend to think that separating into lots and fermenting as such as more precise, instead of taking fruits that are ready together." There's extensive picking—6 passes through Madrona and 3-4 through the other vineyards—and lots that don't make it into the vineyard wines go into a general blend, below that it's sold off in bulk. "I don't get inspiration from Napa I get it from Bordeaux," says Brad. Thorevilos is the most approachable, Capella is the most refined, Howell surprisingly soft at first ("Howell Mountain doesn't have to be hard") until the structure kicks in, and Madrona is the most profound complete ("What you see about Madrona is the beautiful lively backbone.") For me it has the freshness of Cabernet Franc and the backbone of Cabernet Sauvignon. "California in a Bordeaux style," was the comment of a Bordeaux winemaker at a tasting.

Araujo Estate ★★

Calistoga, CA

(1) 707 942 6061

wine@araujoestate.com

www.araujoestate.com

Napa Valley

Eiesele

Altagracia

37 acres; 50,000 bottles

Within a protected canyon east of Calistoga, the Eisele Vineyard has a distinguished history. Named for the Eisele's, who owned it during the 1970s and 1980s, the grapes were initially used to make wine for home consumption. Paul Draper of Ridge Vineyards made the first commercial release in 1971; this was the one and only vintage of Ridge Eisele. In 1972 and 1973 the grapes were sold to Mondavi (reportedly for the Reserve Cabernet Sauvignon). In 1974, Conn Creek Winery produced the second vineyard-labeled release, and then from 1975 the grapes were sold to Joseph Phelps, who produced a vineyard-designated wine until 1991. After the property was purchased by Bart and Daphne Araujo (who as Bordeaux collectors were committed to Cabernet Sauvignon), they made the wine at the estate. It's difficult to compare the Cabernet from Eisele before and after 1991 given vintage variation and differences in age, but it's interesting that in the one year that both Phelps and Araujo released an Eisele bottling, the wines today show more similarities than differences. The Araujo shows more complex, attractive fruits and is more open; the style of the Phelps is more reserved (in line with earlier Eisele vintages and with their Insignia blend of the period). A savory aromatic thread, somewhat reminiscent of the French garrigue, runs through both wines, giving an impression that the vineyard is expressing its terroir. The vineyard was heavily virused so the Araujos started an extensive replanting program, but the virusing prevented using selection massale. However, some years earlier, Shafer's home vineyard had been planted with cuttings from Eisele, and Shafer returned the favor with cuttings that were propagated to make the "young" Eisele selection. Cuttings from Eisele were later cured of viruses, and became the "old" Eisele selection. After twenty years, the original vines are now being replanted. The property has 70 ha, and 15 ha are planted out of 16 plantable hectares. Most is Cabernet Sauvignon, but there are blocks of Merlot, Petit Verdot, Cabernet Franc, Syrah, Sauvignon Blanc, and Viognier. The estate is run on biodynamic principles, including respecting phases of the moon, and there are cows and chickens on the hill behind the vineyards; olive oil and honey are produced in addition to wine. In the early days, the Phelps Eisele was 100% Cabernet Sauvignon, as were the first two Araujo vintages, but since then the wine has been a blend, usually 85-95% Cabernet Sauvignon with some Cabernet Franc and Petit Verdot, sometimes also a little Merlot. Since 1999 there has been a second wine, Altagracia, also based on a Bordeaux blend, but which fluctuates more widely in varietal composition, from 58% to 100% Cabernet Sauvignon. As true with second wines elsewhere, some blocks usually go into Eisele or into Altagracia, but "You can never tell," says winemaker Nigel Kinsman, "in the unusually wet vintage of 2011, some blocks that usually under perform gave the best results." Vinification is conventional, with relatively extended maceration times, about 35-50 days maceration in total. "I believe in getting everything from the skins that they have to offer," says Nigel. Three quarters of plantings are Cabernet Sauvignon and other Bordeaux varieties, but in addition there are varietal Syrah, Sauvignon Blanc, and Viognier. Michel Rolland is consulting winemaker and visits regularly to advise on blending. In 2013, the estate was sold to François Pinault of Château Latour; it's not yet clear whether and what changes this will entail.

Beaulieu Vineyards

1960 Saint Helena Highway, Rutherford, CA 94573

(1) 707 967 5205

info@bv-wine.com

www.bvwines.com

Napa Valley

Napa, Private Reserve, Cabernet Sauvignon

1099 acres; 8,400,000 bottles

Perhaps it's no more than sentimental to include Beaulieu in a list of top Cabernet producers, but it has played such a significant role in the history of Cabernet Sauvignon in Napa Valley. After George de Latour established Beaulieu in the historic heart of Rutherford, the Private Reserve was one of a mere handful of top quality wines made in Napa Valley. André Tchelist-cheff, who made the wine from 1938 until his retirement in 1973, became a legend. Although erratic because there were two bottlings, one brilliant and one not so good, the 1974 was one of the top wines of that legendary vintage. But Beaulieu turned away from quality under the ownership of Heublein, beginning its expansion into the broader market; sold on in 1987, it's now just one of Diageo's labels. The tasting room is in a historic building, but the modern winery behind more resembles an oil refinery. The Private Reserve today is a workmanlike Cabernet, but does not have that special refinement of the historic classic vintages. This is not surprising considering that the plots in the To Kalon vineyard that had been part of the great Private Reserves were sold to Andy Beckstoffer (from whom several producers now purchase grapes for bottlings of cult Cabernets). There are several ranges of wines at quality levels extending to the entry-level BV Coastal Estates (named for their origin in the Central Coast). The wines are well made and serviceable.

Bell Wine Cellars

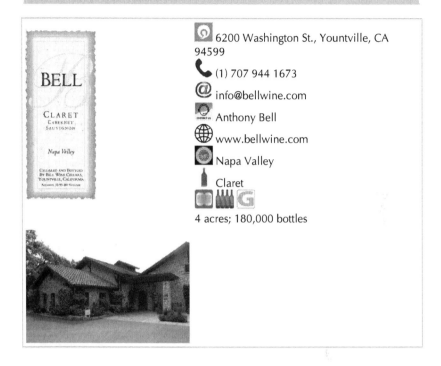

6200 Washington St., Yountville, CA 94599

(1) 707 944 1673

info@bellwine.com

Anthony Bell

www.bellwine.com

Napa Valley

Claret

4 acres; 180,000 bottles

After spending the 1980s at Beaulieu Vineyards, Anthony Bell started his own winery in 1991 by producing Cabernet Sauvignon from clone 6 in borrowed facilities, moving into his own winery in Yountville in 1998. His style is to make wines with a European sensibility. Today he produces monovarietal Cabernet Sauvignons from several different clones, as well as a blend with the classic Bordeaux varieties, and a "claret" that also includes some Syrah and Petite Syrah. Three barrels for each individual clone give around 900 bottles for each of clones 7, 4, 6, and 337. The wines from clone 7 and clone 4 have similar profiles, but on clone 7 you see the fruits first, and this reverses on clone 4 where you see the herbal influence first. All the wines show an impressive sense of the tradition of Cabernet Sauvignon, but the most striking difference is between clone 337, which shows the most lush character—the Dijon clone of Cabernet Sauvignon, you might say—and clone 6, which has the most traditional austerity. The main focus here is on the 6 cuvées of pure varietal Cabernet Sauvignons, but there are also Merlot, Syrah, Chardonnay, and Sauvignon Blanc.

Bryant Family Vineyard ★★★

1567 Sage Canyon Rd., Saint Helena, CA 94574-9628

(1) 314 231 8066

info@bryantwines.com

Brady Mitchell

http://www.bryantwines.com

Napa Valley

Bryant

Bettina

DB4

12 acres; 50,000 bottles

Don Bryant purchased the land for his vineyards in a striking spot on Pritchard Hill overlooking Lake Hennessy. "I bought the top of a mountain for a home site and decided it would be fun to start a vineyard. I looked for the best vineyard within 10-15 miles of the house. There was a vineyard close by, planted with Cabernet Sauvignon and Chardonnay, and run down. All the old winemakers said it was the best vineyard around. Grapes had previously been sold to Caymus and others. I made an unsolicited bid in 1986 for 12 acres, and closed the deal within 24 hours," he recollects. The first vintage was in 1992, with Helen Turley as the winemaker. Early vintages were propelled into instant success. Since then, there have been several winemakers, with changes in style depending on techniques from barrel fermentation to greater maceration and extraction. "Helen's wines were very reflective of vintage, perfumed and delicate in 1996, massive in 1997," says a later winemaker, Helen Keplinger. The vineyard is divided into 22 blocks spread out over 5 ha, and is planted exclusively with Cabernet Sauvignon (a mixture of Spottswoode clone and 337). The vineyards are on west-facing volcanic soils, with a cooling influence from the lake just below. Bryant's character is maintained by declassifying lots into a second wine, called DB4. "Wines that are declassified to DB4 are less concentrated, and the tannins are less refined. DB4 is not necessarily shorter lived than Bryant," says Helen Keplinger. Both Bryant and DB4 are 100% Cabernet Sauvignon. Since 2009 there has been a Bordeaux blend, called Bettina after Don's wife, coming from David Abreu's vineyards at Madrona Ranch, Thorevilos, and Lucia Howell Mountain. Bettina is produced in roughly the same quantity as Bryant (around 1,500 cases).

Caymus Vineyards

**

 8700 Conn Creek Road, P.O. Box 268, Rutherford, CA 94573

📞 (1) 707 963 4204

@ reception@caymus.com

Janet Thomas

🌐 caymus.com

⊙ Napa Valley

Napa Valley

Special Selection

59 acres; 360,000 bottles

The Wagners have been involved in growing grapes in Napa for a long time. "Napa was a different place when we started in the 1880s, then we had phylloxera and Prohibition, and that put the family out of the business. They planted a litany of crops, the best was prunes, so I grew up around prunes and prune dehydration. In 1966 my father pulled up the prunes and planted grapes," recalls Chuck Wagner. Caymus Vineyards started in 1972 with a release of 240 cases of Cabernet Sauvignon. Today Wagner has expanded into a group of family businesses, with wineries all over Napa Valley. At Caymus there are two Cabernets: the Napa Valley bottling and Special Selection, which has been made most years since 1975 by selecting about a quarter of the best lots. Special Selection can come from any of the eight AVAs in which Caymus own or lease vineyards. It's usually 25% from mountain areas and 75% from the valley, but there's wide variation in sources depending on annual conditions. The style changed in the late nineties to become riper and richer, and since 2008 has included about 15% Merlot. Unlike some of the prominent Napa Valley Cabernets, Special Selection is made in good quantities, typically around 15,000 cases. House style is definitely on the rich side. Caymus Napa Cabernet shows strong aromatic overtones of high-toned fruits, but when you go to Special Select, the aromatics become less obtrusive but the intensity on the palate deepens. Caymus is rich but Special Select is smoother and deeper. The Wagners also make Conundrum, which started as an entry-level white wine, blended from several varieties, sourced all over California; more recently a red has been added, made in a crowd-pleasing style that's very different from Caymus. There's also a Napa Valley Zinfandel.

Chappellet Vineyard **

🌐 1581 Sage Canyon Road, Saint Helena, CA 94574

📞 (1) 707 963 7136

@ winery@chappellet.com

🌐 www.chappellet.com

Napa Valley

🍾 Signature

🍾 Pritchard Hill

101 acres

Chappellet is pretty venerable as one of the first wineries to be built in Napa after Prohibition, in 1967 (one year after Mondavi). Driving up the narrow access road from Lake Hennessy, deep into the woods, it feels quite inaccessible. Vineyards aren't visible until you go around to the back of the pyramid-like winery. Covering 700 acres, the estate extends well beyond the vineyards. Grapes are also purchased from some neighboring vineyards. There were already vines on the property when it was purchased, but they were mostly Chenin Blanc. Following a replanting program in the nineties, most of the vineyard today is Cabernet Sauvignon. There are two distinct Cabernet Sauvignon wines: Signature and Pritchard Hill. "The style has evolved but the goal has always been to make bold, fruity, wine. Signature was really designed to be ready; it has as much structure as any Cabernet to age, but we do try to reign in the tannins rather than have a heavy brooding style," says Ry Richards. "Pritchard Hill has a different stylistic objective: more extract, bigger tannins, pure black fruit, boysenberries, espresso coffee, a higher density overall." Signature comes from the estate and east-facing hillsides in the vicinity; the Pritchard Hill bottling is based on selection, and has been an estate wine from 2012. Signature uses 50-60% new oak, and Pritchard Hill has 100%. Both wines are blends with just over 75% Cabernet Sauvignon; both also have Petit Verdot and Malbec but there is Merlot only in Signature. There are 7,000 cases of Signature and 1,500 cases of Pritchard Hill. Beyond Cabernet, there's a full range of wines, mostly varietals.

Colgin Cellars **⋆⋆**

CABERNET SAUVIGNON NAPA VALLEY

colgin

2010

TYCHSON HILL VINEYARD

PO Box 254, Saint Helena, CA 94574

(1) 707 963 0999

info@colgincellars.com

Allison Tauzie

www.colgincellars.com

Napa Valley

Tychson Hill

IX Estate

Cariad

34 acres; 36,000 bottles

One of the estates that created the cult wine movement, Colgin started with the 1992 vintage of Cabernet Sauvignon from the Herb Lamb vineyard (on the outskirts of Howell Mountain), when Helen Turley sourced the grapes from 14 rows in the most exposed position at the top. Herb Lamb continued to be a signature wine until the vineyard had to be replanted in 2008 (it is no longer made). Two other wines come from vineyards around St. Helena. Ann Colgin purchased the Tychson Hill vineyard in 1995, and the first vintage was 2000; located at the north end of St. Helena, it was part of Freemark Abbey (but had collapsed during Prohibition and never been replanted). This is almost pure Cabernet Sauvignon. There's also the Cariad Bordeaux Blend, about half Cabernet Sauvignon, produced since 1999 from a blend between David Abreu's Madrona Ranch and Thorevilos vineyard. The IX Estate on Pritchard Hill, where all wine is now made, was purchased in 1998; it takes its name from the fact that it was lot #9 on Long Ranch Road. It was planted with a traditional Bordeaux mix of varieties, with about two thirds Cabernet Sauvignon; the estate of 80 ha has 8 ha of vineyards, planted on east-facing slopes to catch the morning sun. The first vintage was 2002. In addition to the IX Estate Bordeaux blend, there's a small amount of Syrah. Focus is exclusively on high-end reds. Production of all wines is small: 1,200-1,500 cases of IX Estate, 250 cases of Tychson Hill, 500 cases of Cariad, and (previously) 500 cases of Herb Lamb. Some change of style is evident over the years in the direction of greater refinement. Winemaker Allison Tauziet says any difference is due less to changes of vineyard source than to technical advances. "The biggest difference is the increased precision in viticulture. In the early years when we were making wine from Herb Lamb it was very rudimentary in the vineyard and vinification was in a custom crush," she points out. Current vintages are developing slowly: my concern is the pace with which flavor variety will develop.

Corison Winery ★★

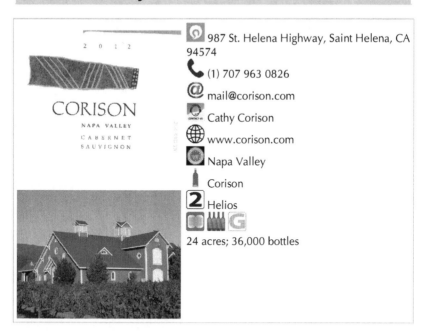

987 St. Helena Highway, Saint Helena, CA 94574

(1) 707 963 0826

mail@corison.com

Cathy Corison

www.corison.com

Napa Valley

Corison

2 Helios

24 acres; 36,000 bottles

Cathy Corison has been fascinated with wine ever since she took a wine appreciation course in college; based on French wine, the course defined her reference point as European. She came to Napa in the early seventies and made wine at Chappellet through the eighties. She first made her own wine from purchased grapes, and continued to make wine for other producers until 2003. The story behind the creation of her winery in Rutherford is that she was determined to find gravelly terroir for her Cabernet Sauvignon, and this turned up in the form of a neglected vineyard in Rutherford, with Bale gravelly loam. There had been plans to develop the site but they had fallen through. This is the basis for her Kronos Cabernet Sauvignon, with vines (most likely clone 7) that were planted on St. George rootstock about forty years ago. Yields are punishingly low, as not only are the vines old, but the vineyard is infected with leaf roll virus. The extra concentration makes the Kronos Cabernet full and plush. The Corison Cabernet Sauvignon is a monovarietal bottling, blended from three vineyards in the Rutherford-St. Helena area (some leased, one of which Cathy was recently able to purchase: "It's a big relief to secure the grapes and have complete control," she says). Corison Cabernet tends to come out around 14% alcohol, Kronos is usually closer to 13%. New oak is about 50%. Graceful aging is a major stylistic objective. "Aging is very important to me. It's almost a moral imperative to make wines that will have a life," Cathy says. Indeed, the wines age slowly; at a vertical tasting in 2012, my favorite was the oldest in the tasting, the 2001. Since then the style seems to have become richer, as typified by the relatively powerful 2012, but a good acidic backbone keeps this in the traditional of ageworthy Cabernets. Production is about 400 cases of Kronos, and about 2,000 cases of Corison Cabernet. Beyond that, the winery has branched out to offer Cabernet Franc, a rosé from Cabernet Sauvignon, and a Gewürztraminer.

Diamond Creek ★★

1599 Diamond Mountain Road, Calistoga, CA 94515

(1) 707 942 6926

info@diamondcreekvineyards.com

www.diamondcreekvineyards.com

Diamond Mountain District

Red Rock

Gravelly Meadow

22 acres; 20,000 bottles

No one had planted vineyards this far north in the mountains when Al Brounstein purchased forested land on Diamond Mountain to create a vineyard in 1968, following a visit to the property with André Tchelistcheff and Louis Martini. Al was not happy with the quality of the Cabernet material that was available in California, but three of the first growths in Bordeaux sold him cuttings, which he then smuggled in by flying privately through Mexico. He was under pressure to plant on AxR1 but stuck to the St George rootstock because it had had a good record in the mountains. He intended to emulate Bordeaux, and also planted Cabernet Franc, Merlot, and Malbec for the blend. There are three individual vineyards, all with roughly the same blend of Cabernet Sauvignon, Merlot, and Cabernet Franc; Petit Verdot comes from a separate plot nearby. Gravelly Meadow is dry farmed, and the other vineyards have irrigation supplied by wells on the property, which has a small lake and a series of waterfalls. All the vineyards were planted at the same time, but Red Rock and Volcanic Hill started producing in 1972, whereas Gravelly Meadow did not produce until 1974. The oldest vines today date from 1988; Red Rock and Gravelly Meadow have more younger vines from a replanting program in the nineties. All vines have been propagated from the original selection, using a nursery on the property. A significant part of the difference between the vineyards is in the tannic structure—taut for Volcanic Hill, elegant for Red Rock, earthy for Gravelly Meadow—so will the characteristic differences between the wines narrow as the tannins resolve with age? I tasted all three vineyards from 1994 to see whether the differences among current vintages were still evident after twenty years. With the moderate alcohol of the early nineties (12.5%), and delicately balanced palates, these were clearly all food wines, with some convergence in style compared to younger vintages. The fruit spectrum was similar in all three, just a touch more aromatic than you would find in Bordeaux of the period, but there were indeed differences in the tannic structure, although not exactly what I expected based on the younger vintages. Volcanic Hill seemed the most mature, savory elements mingling with lightening fruits; Gravelly Meadow seemed the most precise and elegant, a tribute to the conventional wisdom that gravel goes with Cabernet; and Red Rock showed the most evident tannic structure. "Al thought Volcanic Hill would be the longest lived wine, but actually they all age equally well. But Volcanic always comes around last, there is no doubt about that," says Phil Ross. Production is small, around 500 cases each, except for only 100 cases of Lake when it is made. I could not say I have a favorite: in some vintages I prefer Volcanic Hill, and in others Gravelly Meadow. The winery remains committed to exclusively producing Cabernet blends.

Domaine Chandon Winery

📍 1 California Drive, Yountville, CA 94599

📞 (707) 944-2892

@ customerservice@chandon.com

🌐 www.chandon.com

Napa Valley

Etoile

🚶 G

938 acres

Moët & Chandon have expanded out of Champagne to establish subsidiaries in all corners of the globe. The first Chandon Estate was created in Argentina (1960), followed by Napa Valley (1973), Brazil (1973), Australia (1986), Nashik (India, 2013), and Ningxia (China, 2013). The Napa estate is located just outside of Yountville and was one of the first wineries in the area to make tourism a focus, with a astringing room and high-flying restaurant (now closed to make room for expanding the tasting room). Chandon has 135 acres of vineyards around the winery, another vineyard on top of Mt. Veeder (overlooking the town of Napa) at 1,800 ft elevation, and 800 acres in Carneros. The focus is on the classic varieties of Champagne, Pinot Noir, Pinot Meunier, and Chardonnay. Initially there was basically a standard Brut and a special cuvée, Etoile, but now there are also rosé, Blanc de Noirs, Blanc de Blancs, single vineyard wines, and some limited editions. There is no vintage-dated wine in distribution, but small runs from individual years are available at the winery (together with some other small production wines). Still wines are about 10% of sales. The style is richer than Champagne, a little softer and plumper.

Dominus Estate

***

2570 Napanook Rd, Yountville, CA 94599

(1) 707 944 8954

kharris@dominusestate.com

Kassidy Harris

www.dominusestate.com

Napa Valley

Dominus

Napanook

123 acres; 130,000 bottles

In 1982, Christian Moueix, owner of Château Pétrus in Pomerol, entered into a partnership to produce wine from the part of the Napanook vineyard that was owned by John Daniel's daughter. Since then Moueix has been trying to reconstruct the vineyard in its entirety, and has almost succeeded—there's just a small strip at the top that is still owned by Domaine Chandon. The first release of Dominus, under the aegis of the John Daniel Society, was in 1983. In 1995, Christian Moueix became sole owner of the vineyard, and in 1996 the winery was constructed under the principle that it should blend invisibly into the landscape. It has an unusual double skin, with an outer construction of stones packed into netting hiding the construction inside—in the valley, it's sometimes called the stealth winery. In 1996, Moueix introduced a second wine, called Napanook after the vineyard, which is produced by declassification. "At this point Dominus became more refined. But Napanook has experienced the same transition over the years towards greater refinement. Napanook is the same wine Dominus was ten years ago, we say among ourselves," says winemaker Tod Mostero. There's no discrimination between the lots up to the point when the wines go into barriques, with the best lots going into new wood; assemblage is nine months later, and Dominus typically gets 40% new oak and Napanook gets 20%. Grapes from a single plot may go into both wines, sometimes coming from opposite sides of the row (harvested separately); Napanook usually comes from the sunny side, Dominus comes from the more restrained shady side. Dominus usually gives a polished, restrained, impression; Dominus is one of the more restrained Cabernets in Napa. Some attitudes come straight from France. "We still make wine that is intended to be aged, you can probably start to drink five years after the harvest, but I consider that it doesn't really begin to become expressive until it's ten years, sometimes twenty," says Tod. Napanook is simpler, more approachable, more obvious. There are 6-7,000 cases of Dominus and 4-5,000 cases of Napanook.

Dunn Vineyards

 805 White Cottage Rd., Angwin, CA 9408

 (1) 707 965 3642

 dunnvineyards@sbcglobal.net

 Mike Dunn

 www.dunnvineyards.com

 Napa Valley

 Howell Mountain

 Napa Valley

34 acres; 50,000 bottles

One of the pioneers of Howell Mountain, Randy Dunn identified his vineyard in 1972 when he was winemaker at Caymus. Today it has expanded from the couple of original hectares to about 14 ha planted in a much larger estate. The winery is a practical construction with some equipment outside, and the barrel room tunneled into the mountain. The original vineyard remains the core source for the Howell Mountain grapes, but is due for replanting soon, as yields have dropped significantly. Wine making is traditional; there's very little manipulation, no sorting of the grapes, stems are retained, and pump-overs are vigorous: "We do what we can to extract as much as possible," says Mike Dunn. The only exception is alcohol: Randy Dunn remains adamant that it must be less than 14%. A program to eliminate Brett, in conjunction with a move to more new oak, lightened the style slightly in 2002. "Before 2002 the optimum age was more than twenty years: now?—give me ten years and we'll see," says Mike Dunn, adding, "I feel the need to repeat that the 'style' hasn't changed except for Brett management, barrel selection, and percent of new barrels." There are two Cabernet Sauvignons: Howell Mountain and

Napa Valley. Since 2009, all the estate wine has gone into the Howell Mountain bottling. The Napa Valley bottling previously included wine from other sources on Howell Mountain as well as from elsewhere in the valley, but since 2009 has been all Howell Mountain, so it has become something of a second wine for declassified lots. In fact, my favorite was the Napa 1990. Production is around 3,000 cases of Howell Mountain and 1,200 cases of Napa Valley.

Far Niente

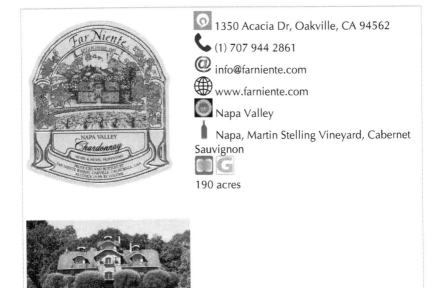

1350 Acacia Dr, Oakville, CA 94562

(1) 707 944 2861

info@farniente.com

www.farniente.com

Napa Valley

Napa, Martin Stelling Vineyard, Cabernet Sauvignon

190 acres

In the heart of Oakville, just across from the famous Martha's Vineyard, Far Niente is an old winery with a gothic building dating from the mid nineteenth century. Approached by a long, elegant drive, it's immediately surrounded by gardens rather than vineyards. The current era of winemaking dates from 1979. The caves underneath the building where the barriques are stored were constructed recently, in stages since 1990. The major source for estate grapes is the Martin Stelling Vineyard, named for a former owner who built up the vineyard but died before it produced grapes. Located just to the west of the winery, running up to the hills of Oakville, it was planted in 1978 with Cabernet Sauvignon and other Bordeaux varieties. Some grapes also come from another vineyard in Oakville. Far Niente has been 100% Oakville since 2001 (previously some grapes came from Coombsville, which is now solely the source for the Chardonnay. The Cabernet Sauvignon is smooth and approachable, with a certain softness to the fruits; the Chardonnay is in a powerful oaky style.

Grgich Hills Cellar

GRGICH HILLS
ESTATE

Napa Valley
FUMÉ BLANC
Dry Sauvignon Blanc
ESTATE 2013 GROWN

1829 Saint Helena Hwy., Rutherford, CA 94573

(1) 800 532 3057

info@grgich.com

www.grgich.com

Napa Valley

Napa, Chardonnay

365 acres

An immigrant from Croatia who arrived in America with nothing but a small suitcase, Mike Grgich was at Beaulieu during the 1960s, and then gained instant fame as the winemaker who crafted the 1973 Chardonnay at Chateau Montelena that won the Judgment of Paris tasting in 1976. Together with a business partner in 1977, he founded his own winery, Grgich Hills, in Rutherford. Today there's a wide range of about ten varietal wines from Grgich Hills; the estate has grown quite large, and since 2003 only estate grapes have been used, coming from vineyards in several locations in Napa Valley. Chardonnay remains Grgich's best known wine; currently it has a powerdul, oaky style. The Cabernet has good structue with its precision giving a sense of minerality.

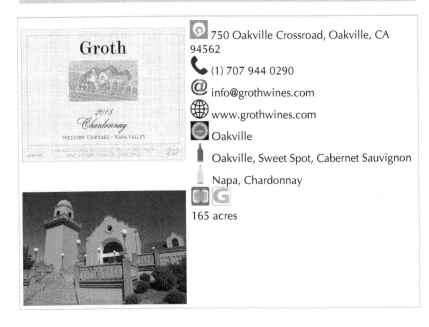

Groth Vineyards & Winery

*

750 Oakville Crossroad, Oakville, CA 94562

(1) 707 944 0290

info@grothwines.com

www.grothwines.com

Oakville

Oakville, Sweet Spot, Cabernet Sauvignon

Napa, Chardonnay

165 acres

Groth is a classic story of a family who moved from other business into owning and running a winery in Napa. Two vineyards on the valley floor were purchased in 1981 and 1982, production began immediately and increased rapidly, and by 1985 the winery was a full time occupation. The striking winery was constructed in 1990 and extended in 2007. The Cabernet and the Reserve Cabernet (from a dedicated block in the vineyard) come from Oakville; the whites are a Chardonnay and Sauvignon Blanc. The Sauvignon Blanc shows a rich style, with exotic fruit notes, the Chardonnay is classic Napa with notes of butter and vanillin adding to the fruits, and the Cabernet has that structured impression of Oakville. The wines offer a good representation of the current character of Napa Valley.

Harlan Estate ★★★

P.O. Box 352, Oakville, CA 94562-0352

(1) 707 944 1441

weaver@harlanestate.com

Summer Jimenez

www.harlanestate.com

Napa Valley

Harlan Estate

2 The Maiden

39 acres; 32,000 bottles

Harlan's hundred hectare estate is a beautiful property in the hills above Oakville, overlooking Martha's Vineyard, To Kalon, and Napanook. After several years searching for land in Napa, Bill Harlan bought the land in tranches, starting in 1984, and planted the vineyards between 1985 and the early 1990s. The estate rises from 60 m to 350 m, with the vineyards planted between 50 m and 160 m. About three quarters of the terroir is volcanic, and one quarter sedimentary. The original vineyards were planted at 1,800 vines/ha, which was considered a relatively high density at the time, but subsequent plantings have moved up to 5,400 vines/ha, and even 7,500 (positively Bordeaux-like). The plantings are a classic Médoc mix, about 70% Cabernet Sauvignon, the rest Merlot, Cabernet Franc, and Petit Verdot. The soils vary from volcanic to sedimentary; Merlot is grown on the sedimentary soils that have better water retention. None of the first three vintages (1987-1989) were sold commercially; the first commercial vintage, 1990, was released in 1996. Michel Rolland is the consulting winemaker. Total production of the estate wine is about 2,000 cases; there are also 600 cases of a second wine, The Maiden. The wines age well: recently my favorite vintage has oscillated between the 1991 and the 1995. Together with winemaker Bob Levy, Bill Harlan started a second operation in 1997; BOND has the same winemaking team, but here the objective is to produce cuvées that express different terroirs, with individual vineyards ranging from 7 to 11 acres in a variety of locations on both sides of the valley. At last count there were five cuvées. I find the style of the BOND cuvées to be noticeably richer than that of Harlan.

Heitz Cellars ******

NAPA VALLEY
CABERNET SAUVIGNON
PRODUCED AND BOTTLED IN OUR CELLAR BY
HEITZ WINE CELLARS
ST. HELENA, CALIFORNIA, U.S.A.

500 Taplin Road, Saint Helena, CA 94574

(1) 707 963 3542

cheitz@napanet.net

Kathleen Heitz Myers

www.heitzcellar.com

Napa Valley

Martha's Vineyard

375 acres; 480,000 bottles

Dating from the 1960s, Heitz is now regarded as one of the venerable old Napa producers. From its first vintage in 1968, Heitz Martha's Vineyard was regarded as a benchmark for Napa Cabernet; the 1974 is still regarded as one of the best wines ever made in California. However, an infection in the winery with TCA made the vintages from 1985 questionable (the 1987 was the worst affected), and it took several years for the problem to be recognized; the wines did not become completely free of cork taint until 1992. And then the vineyard had to be replanted because of phylloxera, so there was no vintage in 1995; the wine came from relatively young vines for the rest of the decade. Has Martha's Vineyard ever fully recovered its reputation? Some recent vintages suggest a road to recovery; others seem to have lost their way entirely. In addition to its most famous wine, there are two other single vineyard Cabernets, Bella Oaks (in Rutherford) and Trailside (on the other side of the valley by the Silverado Trail). Heitz also produces Napa Valley Cabernet, Zinfandel, Chardonnay, and some other single varietal wines, but none has achieved the acclaim of their Cabernet Sauvignons. The style with the single vineyard Cabernets is for quite extended oak aging, with one year in the fermentation cuves of American oak followed by thirty months in French barriques. Certainly there is a similarity of style, especially between Bella Oaks and Martha's Vineyard, although Martha's Vineyard is always the most intense, and needs the most time to come around. I still don't think any subsequent vintage has equaled the 1974.

Inglenook

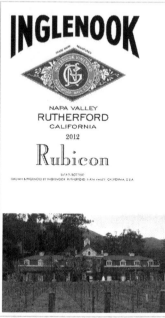

1991 St Helena Highway, Rutherford, CA 94573

707-968-1100

reservations@inglenook.com

https://www.inglenook.com

Napa Valley

Rubicon, Cabernet Sauvignon

The old Inglenook winery at the heart of Rutherford has a chequered history. Some people regard it as the birthplace of fine wine, or at least of fine wine based on Cabernet Sauvignon, in Napa. Finnish sea captain Gustave Niebaum, who made a fortune trading furs in Alaska, decided after a visit to France that the gravelly loam soils of Rutherford resembled Bordeaux and might reward attempts to produce the same blend of wine. He planted Cabernet Sauvignon, together with Cabernet Franc and Merlot. A splendid Gothic mansion was constructed to house winemaking. Inglenook Cabernets were famous in the period after Prohibition. The winery was sold to United Vintners in 1964, and then became part of Heublein when United Vintners was itself sold in 1969. Quality went out of the window. In 1975, film director Francis Ford Coppola purchased Niebaum's former home together with 49 hectares of surrounding vineyards, and then in 1995 Heublein tired of the business and sold him the Inglenook winery and the rest of the vineyards. The house is now a visitor center, and viticulture and vinification have been modernized. The original holdings were reunited under the name Rubicon Estate. The Inglenook name was sold to Constellation, who sold it to The Wine Group in 2008; it was used for jug wine until Coppola got it back in 2011. So the winery is now called Inglenook, and the top wine is called Rubicon (a classic blend with about 86% Cabernet Sauvignon). The second wine was previously called CASK, but now is labeled simply as Inglenook Cabernet Sauvignon (it's a similar blend to Rubicon). The wines are quite mainstream for Napa. There's also Syrah, Zinfandel, Sauvignon Blanc, and a Rhône-style white.

Jarvis Winery

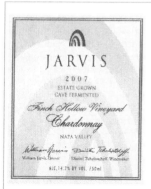

 2970 Monticello Rd, Napa, CA 94558-9615

 (1) 800 255 5280

 wines@jarvisnapa.com

www.jarviswines.com

Napa Valley

Cabernet Sauvignon Reserve

37 acres; 85,000 bottles

The creation of William Jarvis, whose career was in Silicon Valley, Jarvis has a rather unusual facility, a bunker cut into the mountain (using the equipment that created the Channel tunnel between England and France). The tunnel curves around in a large circle, with rooms off to the side and tanks and vats along the way. Well to the east of Napa Valley proper, vineyards are at 1,000 foot elevation and are around 6 degrees cooler than the valley floor. There are several separate vineyards occupying 37 planted acres out of a total estate of 1320 acres. Fermentation is all in stainless steel, with some rotary tanks used for Cabernet Sauvignon and Cabernet Franc. MLF is performed in large wooden cuves, then the wine goes into barrels. Production is only estate wine; the first vintage was 1992. The focus is on Cabernet Sauvignon, using one of the clones that performed best in the trials at Beaulieu, giving low yields. Most of the wines are single varietals, particularly Cabernet Sauvignon, Cabernet Franc, Merlot, and Chardonnay. The Reserve designation is used for the top wines, which are barrel selections. The Lake William cuvée was created by accident when William Jarvis pumped Cabernet Franc into a tank of Cabernet Sauvignon. Consulting winemaker Dimitri Tchelistcheffwas very cross, until it turned out that the wine was actually rather successful, and it has now become a regular bottling in the range. the Cabernet Sauvignon has quite a restrained style, The Reserve has more density and chocolate notes, the Lake William actually seems more tightly structured, and the top Chardonnay, Finch Hollow, tends towards the exotic.

Joseph Phelps Vineyards **

200 Taplin Road, Saint Helena, CA 94574

(1) 707 963 2745

preferred@josephphelps.com

www.josephphelps.com

Napa Valley

Backus

Napa Valley

Insignia

380 acres; 600,000 bottles

Insignia is one of California's most genuine cult wines, meaning that it is produced in appreciable quantities (up to 20,000 cases), roughly comparable to a Bordeaux château. As a selection of the best cuvées, it should represent the best of the vintage, but at these quantities should still be strongly influenced by general vintage character. It has been a Cabernet-dominated blend since the 1980s, averaging around 80% Cabernet Sauvignon, with the remainder coming from all the other Bordeaux varieties in varying proportions. The grapes originate in about six vineyard plots, in various parts of Napa Valley. Vintage 2003 was the last year in which any grapes came from growers: today the wine is entirely an estate production. The wine is not easy to judge when young, given the powerful fruits, which take ten years or more, depending on vintage, to resolve enough to allow complexity to show. I am inclined to divide the Insignias into two series. There's a lineage of vintages 1997, 2001, 2007, which seems more European in balance and restraint; there's an alternative lineage from 1999, 2002, 2008, which shows more overt fruit and aromatics in the New World style. The differences are evident in pairwise comparisons: 1997 versus 1999, 2001 versus 2002, 2007 versus 2008. I could not see any direct correlation with varietal composition, which changes in order to maintain consistency of style, and it therefore seems that the differences reflect vintage character, which is as it should be. Phelps remains one of the most reliable producers in Napa. It has expanded significantly, with vineyards in Sonoma as well as various locations in Napa Valley, and Pinot Noir, Sauvignon Blanc, and Viognier also in its line up.

Louis Martini Winery ★★

254 South Saint Helena Highway, Saint Helena, CA 94574

(1) 707 963 2736

info@louismartini.com

www.louismartini.com

Napa Valley

Monte Rosso

1,200,000 bottles

One of the oldest established wine producers in California, Louis Martini had its origins when the first Louis started making wine at the beginning of the twentieth century, and somewhat unusually formed his own company during Prohibition to produce sacramental wine and kits for home wine-making. At the end of Prohibition he built a winery in St. Helena. In 1938 he expanded into Sonoma by purchasing the Goldstein Ranch (originally planted in the 1880s), which he renamed Monte Rosso. In 1951 his son, also Louis Martini, took over winemaking, and in 1977 the third genera-tion, Michael Martini, took over. The winery and vineyards were sold to Gallo in 2002. The best known vineyard in Sonoma, Monte Rosso is re-nowned for both its old Zinfandel and Cabernet Sauvignon. Today there are 25 ha of Zinfandel, 40 ha of Cabernet Sauvignon, and 6 ha of Petite Syrah or other varieties. There are two blocks of white grapes. Martini pro-duces several wines from Monte Rosso. The most famous is probably the gnarly vine Zinfandel, which comes from some of the oldest plantings, followed by the (100%) Cabernet Sauvignon. A special blend called Los Ninos was produced from 1979, initially as a Cabernet, then becoming a

Meritage after 1985; the blend included Petit Verdot for the first few years and from 2001 had Cabernet Franc as the other variety. In 2008 Martini introduced a Proprietary Red, which is more than half Petit Verdot with one third Cabernet Sauvignon. Martini's general production is more or less standard for Napa, but Monte Rosso really is a special representation of Sonoma.

Chateau Montelena ★★

🔍 1429 Tubbs Lane, Calistoga, CA 94515

📞 (1) 707 942 5105

@ reservations@montelena.com

👤 Jeff Adams

🌐 www.montelena.com

◉ Napa Valley

🍾 Napa Valley, Chardonnay

🍾 Cabernet Sauvignon, Montelena Estate

2 Cabernet Sauvignon

🚶 G

247 acres; 400,000 bottles

Chateau Montelena is that rare thing in California: a real chateau, origi-nally called the A. L. Tubbs Winery after its founder , who constructed it in 1888. Jim Barrett bought the property and vineyard and revived it from its dilapidated state to start making wine in 1972. Today the wine is made by Jim's son, Bo Barrett. Although Chateau Montelena won the Judgment of Paris for its Chardonnay, its Cabernet Sauvignon was one of the trendset-ters through the 1970s. This has now become the Montelena Estate bottling, sourced from the vineyards around the winery at the very north-ern limit of Napa Valley. The elevation is around 120 m, which no doubt compensates for the increase in temperature that's usually found going up the valley. The wine is a blend from several sites that ripen over a 4-6 week period, increasing complexity. It has a long and distinguished reputa-tion for elegance. But there is also another, completely different, Cabernet Sauvignon, also under the Napa Valley appellation, which comes from other vineyards and is made in a much simpler style. The only distinction between them on the bottle is a gold band stating "The Montelena Estate" on the original bottling. It would be easy to become confused. Personally, I like the older vintages better than the more powerful recent vintages; the 1985 was still going strong in 2012. Neither the white nor red shows New World exuberance; the style is relatively restrained, but there's a tendency in more recent vintages for the wines to tighten up and become leaner, losing that flush of youthful fruit that makes them so attractive.

Opus One   ★★★

7900 Saint Helena Hwy, Oakville, CA 94562

(1) 707 944 9442

info@opusonewinery.com

Michael Silacci

www.opusonewinery.com

Napa Valley

Napa Valley

Ouverture

167 acres; 300,000 bottles

Created as a joint venture between Robert Mondavi and Baron Philippe de Rothschild in 1979, Opus One was one of the first collaborations between Bordeaux and Napa winemakers. Before Opus One had its own vineyards, grapes came from Mondavi's holding of To Kalon, so the first vintage in 1979 was really more of a super-cuvée than Opus One as it later developed. The wine was made at Mondavi until Opus One's winery was constructed in 1991. Across route 29 from Mondavi, the Opus One winery is a somewhat bunker-like building nestled into the hillside. The first estate vineyard was established when Mondavi sold the 14 ha Q block of the To Kalon vineyard to the new venture. Further vineyards directly across route 29 were purchased in 1983 and 1984, and another 19 ha of To Kalon were transferred after Constellation took over Mondavi in 2004. Over the years the vineyards have been steadily replanted at higher vine density with lower-yielding clones, and they now appear more European. After Constellation Brands acquired Mondavi, Opus One became completely independent. "The dissolution of the partnership (between the owners of Opus One) was a catalyst for change," says Michael Silacci. "This is more of an independent operation now." There is now also a second wine, Ouverture, available at the winery, produced from lots that are declassified from Opus One; it is described as "less structured than Opus One and more approachable in its youth." Production is less than 12%, and it is not vintage-dated. "The assumption from the beginning was that there should be a Bordeaux blend," says Michael Silacci, but there's always a high content of Cabernet Sauvignon (usually over 85%). Initially the blend started with Cabernet Franc and Merlot; Malbec was added in 1994 and Petit Verdot was added in 1997. The wine is easy to underrate in the early years, when it tends to be somewhat dumb, and to retain a touch of austerity. In terms of aging, the 2005 is showing beautifully now, and the 1995 shows the extra elegance of another decade's age. The very first vintage remains vibrant today.

Philip Togni Vineyard

PHILIP TOGNI
Vineyard

2001
Napa Valley
CABERNET SAUVIGNON   Estate Bottled

Spring Mountain Rd, Saint Helena, CA 94574

(1) 707 963 3731

tognivyd@wildblue.net

Philip Togni

www.philiptognivineyard.com

Napa Valley

Philip Togni

2 Tanbark

24 acres; 24,000 bottles

Philip Togni was first involved in planting Cabernet Sauvignon in 1959, and worked in a variety of countries before coming to Cuvaison in Napa. He was involved with several mountain vineyards, including Pride and Chappellet (he made the 1969 Chappellet Cabernet, which is considered on of the great successes of the decade), before he started to clear the land for his own vineyard in 1975, when he planted the first 3 acres of Sauvignon Blanc, followed by 1.5 acres of Cabernet Franc in 1981, all on AxR1. By 1985 everything had been replanted on 110 rootstock. The estate is at the top of Spring Mountain, close to the border between Napa and Sonoma. It's set well back from the road, and you are given detailed instructions on how to find the unmarked driveway (and to lock the gate behind you). Philip's daughter Lisa is now slowly taking over the winemaking. There are three lines of wines: Togni estate, Tanbark (a second label, introduced pretty much right at the beginning, in 1986), and Ca'Togni (only for sweet wine made from Black Hamburg). "We started off saying we wanted to make a Médoc wine," Philip says, and his Cabernet Sauvignon is typically about 86% Cabernet Sauvignon, with the rest from the other three Bordeaux varieties. Merlot is a little under represented in the wine (6%) compared to plantings (15%) because its yields are lower than the other varieties. The current vintage, together with ten year old wines from a library, is offered to subscribers in the Fall. The wines are intended for the long haul.

Pride Mountain Vineyards

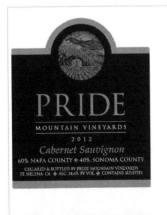

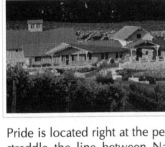

4026 Spring Mountain Road, Saint Helena, CA 94574

(1) 707 963 4949

contactus@pridewines.com

Sally Johnson

www.pridewines.com

Napa Valley

Reserve Claret

Vintner Select

California

83 acres; 200,000 bottles

Pride is located right at the peak of Spring Mountain. In fact, the vineyards straddle the line between Napa and Sonoma (one inconvenient consequence being that regulations require two bonded wineries, one for handling Napa wines, the other for Sonoma). The origin of every lot has to be tracked. If a wine has more than 75% of grapes from Napa, it can be labeled with the Napa AVA, but most wines carry complicated accounts of the percent coming from Napa County versus Sonoma County. Vineyards are around 700 m, above the fog line, with 60% on the Sonoma side. Plantings are mostly Bordeaux varieties, with a little Syrah and small amounts of Chardonnay and Viognier. There are three different Cabernet Sauvignons and also a "Claret." The largest production, around 5,000 cases, is the Estate Cabernet Sauvignon, which usually has a bit more fruit from Napa than Sonoma. Winemaker Sally Johnson says this is at its peak for drinking about one year after release, although personally I'd prefer to wait another year. The two higher tiers are Vintner Select (500-600 cases) and the Reserve Cabernet Sauvignon (1,200 cases). "Vintner Select is the epitome of the California style, flashy and showy, it's 100% Napa," says Sally. It's a 100% Cabernet Sauvignon exclusively from clone 337. The

Reserve is a more masculine wine intended for longer aging. "Not many people are making wines like the Reserve," she says. This sometimes has a couple of percent Petit Verdot, and is dominated by Pride's own Rock Arch clone of Cabernet Sauvignon. There's also the Reserve Claret, which is a Merlot-Cabernet Sauvignon blend.

Robert Foley

Summit Lake Drive, Angwin, CA 94508

(707) 965-2669

Bob@RobertFoleyVineyards.com

www.robertfoleyvineyards.com

Napa Valley

Napa Valley

Bob Foley started working for Heitz in the 1970s, moved to Markham, and then to Pride, and altogether has made 35 vintages in Napa. He started Robert Foley in 1998, with a single wine called Claret. He gained more access to vineyards over the following years, planted his own vineyard, and Claret graduated into a 100% Cabernet because they started bottling the Merlot separately. Until 2003 the wine was a blend, from 2004 to 2005 it had 7% Merlot, since 2006 it has been 100% Cabernet Sauvignon. Production was 500 cases when he started, today it is 8,000 altogether, but it's still a two person company. With 2010 he has gone back to a Bordeaux blend for Claret and will have a separate Cabernet bottling. He is fussy about clones: "Clones of Cabernet are very important. I work with three main clones: the two old clones 4 and 7 are my favorites for masculinity. The newest clone I work with (since 1992) is 337 for its femininity," he says.

Robert Mondavi Winery

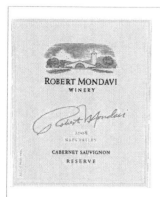

⊚ 7801 Saint Helena Hwy, Oakville, CA 94562

☏ (1) 888 766 6328

@ spotlight@robertmondaviwinery.com

⊕ www.robertmondavi.com

◉ Napa Valley

Robert Mondavi

1000 acres; 2,700,000 bottles

Mondavi scarcely needs any introduction as an icon of Napa Valley. The winery was built in 1966 and the first vintage of Cabernet Sauvignon was released in 1968. A bottling originally called the Unfiltered Cabernet Sauvignon was renamed as the Reserve from 1971; the 1974 Reserve was one of the wines that put Napa Valley Cabernet on the map. The company broadened out with the introduction of the cheaper Woodbridge brand in 1979 from wine made in Lodi. Mondavi continued to be run by the Mondavi family, with Robert's son Tim as winemaker, although it became a publicly quoted company, until it was sold to the conglomerate Constellation for $1.36 billion in 2004. (Tim Mondavi now makes wine at his own, independent company.) Today Mondavi produces three Cabernet Sauvignons. The Napa Valley bottling is dominated by grapes from To Kalon and Stags Leap District (typically around a third each); Cabernet Sauvignon is 75-85% with Cabernet Franc and Merlot as second in importance, and small amounts of Malbec, Petit Verdot, and Syrah. The Oakville bottling is dominated by To Kalon (typically more than three quarters): it has slightly more Cabernet Sauvignon, with Cabernet Franc as the second variety, and small amounts of Merlot, Malbec, and Petit Verdot. The flagship Napa Valley Reserve comes largely (sometimes almost exclusively) from To Kalon. It's usually more than 85% Cabernet Sauvignon; Merlot tended to be the second variety in the early years, but since the mid nineties Cabernet Franc has been second. Petit Verdot made its first appearance in the blend in 1997. In addition, in occasional vintages there is a bottling of a To Kalon Cabernet Sauvignon (from a block of old vines) or a Stags Leap District Cabernet Sauvignon, both 100% varietal. Mondavi also produces Chardonnay, of course, but in some ways is better known for the Fumé Blanc, a Sauvignon Blanc matured in oak barriques; the Reserve To-Kalon bottling has great depth and character, with potential for aging.

Robert Sinskey Vineyards

6320 Silverado Trail, Napa, CA 94558

(1) 707 944 9090

rsv@robertsinskey.com

Rob Sinskey

www.robertsinskey.com

Napa Valley

Carneros, Four Vineyards, Pinot Noir

The modern winery is located on the Silverado Trail in Napa Valley, but the vineyards are in Carneros, where Sinskey has four Pinot Noir vineyards (there is also a vineyard in Sonoma). About half of all production is Pinot Noir, making Sinskey a Pinot Noir specialist in the area. Wines are made only from estate fruit. Until 2001 Sinskey made a Carneros Pinot Noir and a reserve bottling, but felt that "Reserve" had little meaning since the wines were not produced in a rich oaky style, so the change was made to single vineyard bottlings. There is complete destemming for all wines, cap irrigation during fermentation rather than pigeage to give better control of extraction, and maturation in 30% new oak. The wines are intended to drink well from soon after the vintage, and Sinskey says that he sees about ten years as the natural life span for most vintages.

Schrader Cellars

Cabernet Sauvignon   Napa Valley

Schrader
— G I I I —
2009
RUTHERFORD
Beckstoffer Georges III Vineyard
14.4% ALCOHOL BY VOLUME

1345 Lincoln Avenue, Calistoga, CA 94515

(1) 707 942 1212

info@schradercellars.com

www.schradercellars.com

Napa Valley

CCS Cabernet Sauvignon

0 acres; 22,000 bottles

Fred Schrader cofounded Colgin-Schrader Cellars in 1992, and then moved to found Schrader Cellars with his wife Carol in 1998. The present portfolio concentrates on single vineyard bottlings from To Kalon and the George III vineyard. The To Kalon bottlings emphasize small plots within the vineyard, mostly planted with individual clones. The first year of production from To Kalon was 2000, but 2001 was the year when the Schraders moved to an acreage contract, giving them control over issues such as harvesting, which is late, usually at the start of October. The style has always been towards powerful cult wines, ripe, rich, and full, but the massive underlying structure takes them far away from fruit bombs. The characters of the individual bottlings demonstrate the relative differences between the clones at a high level of concentration and ripeness, with clone 6 the most structured, 337 the most opulent, and clone 4 the most loose knit.

Screaming Eagle Winery

***

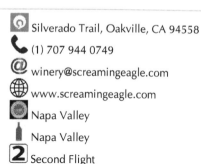

Silverado Trail, Oakville, CA 94558

(1) 707 944 0749

winery@screamingeagle.com

www.screamingeagle.com

Napa Valley

Napa Valley

2 Second Flight

44 acres; 15,000 bottles

Screaming Eagle scarcely needs any introduction: it is by far California's most famous cult wine. The winery was created when Jean Phillips bought 23 ha of land just off the Silverado trail, in the Oakville area, for an unusually high price in 1986. The area was known to the neighbors as providing high quality grapes; largely Riesling, it was replanted to Cabernet Sauvignon in 1987 with small amounts of Merlot and Cabernet Franc. Heidi Barrett was engaged as winemaker. Since then, further replanting, managed by David Abreu, has brought the vineyard into a Bordeaux-like balance of Cabernet Sauvignon, Cabernet Franc, and Merlot. The slight depression in the land creates a small frost problem from time to time, which is handled by overhead sprinklers fed by a lake. Drainage has been installed under the new plantings to recapture water. They expect to dry farm more or less around two thirds of the ranch, especially where there's more clay (to the west). This is an early ripening site, but even so, they are early pickers here, usually a week to ten days ahead of everyone else. The Cabernet has historically been clones 7 and See, but in the last couple of years some clones 6, 169, and 337 have crept in. The winery was sold in 2006 to two partners, one of whom has since left. A new winery was constructed for the 2010 vintage; it's not exactly utilitarian, but certainly focuses directly on winemaking. There's an open barn covering the crush pad, with hatches to allow the grapes to go straight into the fermenters below, where there is an underground facility including all sorts of fermentation tanks. Grapes are usually picked at 24-25 Brix with a pH around 3.5; there is no acidification. There is a total of about 4 weeks on the skins, starting with cold maceration for about 5 days, yeast are added to start fermentation, which lasts 7-10 days, and then there are 2 weeks or more on the skins. Malolactic fermentation is performed in barrel. A little press wine is used most years. They worry a lot about air exposure and try to minimize handling; racking is done under argon. The wine spends about 18 months in French oak. "New oak is about 75%: 100% would be too much," says winemaker Nick Gislason, who is aided by consultant Michel Rolland. Annual production is generally less than 750 cases, and the wine is available only to a member list (with a limit of three bottles per member); the waiting list is several years long. A second wine, called Second Flight, coming from young vines and declassified lots, was introduced in 2012; it varies from a third to a half of total production, and selling for a third to a quarter of the price of Screaming Eagle itself, it is still rather expensive.

Shafer Vineyards

6154 Silverado Trail, Napa, CA 94558

707 944 2877

info@shafervineyards.com

John Gretz

www.shafervineyards.com

Napa Valley

One Point Five

Hillside Select

Napa Valley

205 acres; 384,000 bottles

John Shafer left a career in corporate publishing to move to Napa Valley, where he purchased 210 acres and planted vineyards in 1972 in what became the Stags Leap District in 1989. The first vintage in 1978 used Cabernet Sauvignon from the Sunspot vineyard that rises up immediately above the winery. Hillside Select started in 1983, when Doug Shafer became winemaker. "I was tasting lots and the Sunspot was head and shoulders above everything else. I thought we should bottle it separately—this became the 1982 Reserve. That started the program. I got tired of explaining what Reserve was, because everyone had a reserve, and in 1983 we called it Hillside Select. The fruits are so good you can keep your hands off it—Hillside Select is the easiest wine to make," Doug says. There are about 20 ha on the hillside block, and the best lots are selected each year for Hillside Select, of which there are usually 2,000-2,500 cases. It's 100% Cabernet Sauvignon. There are also about 8,000 cases of the One Point Five Cabernet Sauvignon, which comes from the hillside estate vineyard and the Borderline vineyard two miles south of Shafer at the edge of the Stags Leap District. Other wines include Chardonnay, Merlot, and Syrah. The style is rich and lush, distinctly New World, for all the wines.

Spottswoode Estate Vineyard

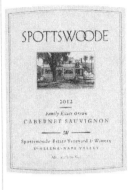

1902 Madrona Avenue, Saint Helena, CA 94574

(1) 707 963 0134

estate@spottswoode.com

Erica Wallenbrock

www.spottswoode.com

Napa Valley

Napa Valley

Lyndenhurst

37 acres; 450,000 bottles

Driving along Madrona Avenue in downtown St. Helena through suburban housing, you wonder where the Spottswoode winery can be, and then suddenly you come out into 15 hectares of vineyards that stretch from the edge of the town up to the mountains. Jack and Mary Novak purchased the property in 1972, and were refused a permit to make wine because the neighborhood was residential. The later purchase (in 1990) of a winery across the road allowed the wine to be made in the vicinity. The Cabernet Sauvignon is a blend, although there is no Merlot. "We don't have any Merlot growing here, I'm not a fan of Merlot in this area. There was some Merlot at Spottswoode long ago, but it was removed," says winemaker Aron Weinkauf. In addition to 12.5 ha of Cabernet Sauvignon, there are 1.25 ha of Cabernet Franc and 0.4 ha of Petit Verdot for the blend, and also a hectare of Sauvignon Blanc. A second wine, called Lyndenhurst, is made in a more approachable fruit-forward, less ageworthy style (using 60% new oak compared to Spottswoode's 68%). Production is usually about 3,000 cases of Spottswoode and 700 cases of Lyndenhurst. My favorite vintage of Spottswoode is the 1992.

Stag's Leap Wine Cellars

5766 Silverado Trail, Napa CA 94558

(1) 707 944 2020

retail@cask23.com

www.cask23.com

Napa Valley

Fay Vineyard, Cabernet Sauvignon

239 acres; 1,800,000 bottles

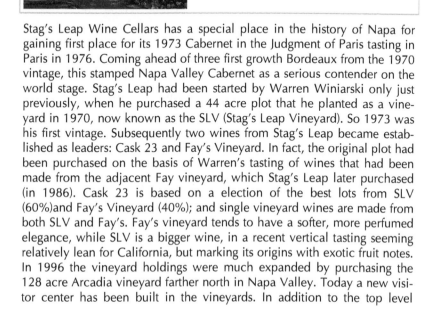

Stag's Leap Wine Cellars has a special place in the history of Napa for gaining first place for its 1973 Cabernet in the Judgment of Paris tasting in Paris in 1976. Coming ahead of three first growth Bordeaux from the 1970 vintage, this stamped Napa Valley Cabernet as a serious contender on the world stage. Stag's Leap had been started by Warren Winiarski only just previously, when he purchased a 44 acre plot that he planted as a vineyard in 1970, now known as the SLV (Stag's Leap Vineyard). So 1973 was his first vintage. Subsequently two wines from Stag's Leap became established as leaders: Cask 23 and Fay's Vineyard. In fact, the original plot had been purchased on the basis of Warren's tasting of wines that had been made from the adjacent Fay vineyard, which Stag's Leap later purchased (in 1986). Cask 23 is based on a election of the best lots from SLV (60%)and Fay's Vineyard (40%); and single vineyard wines are made from both SLV and Fay's. Fay's vineyard tends to have a softer, more perfumed elegance, while SLV is a bigger wine, in a recent vertical tasting seeming relatively lean for California, but marking its origins with exotic fruit notes. In 1996 the vineyard holdings were much expanded by purchasing the 128 acre Arcadia vineyard farther north in Napa Valley. Today a new visitor center has been built in the vineyards. In addition to the top level wines, there's also a mid-level range under the name of Napa Valley Collection and a line or cheaper wines under the Hawk Crest label. In 2007, the winery was sold to a partnership of Chateau Ste. Michelle and Antinori, and since then has somewhat lost its luster. Recent vintages of SLV have been awfully soft for a wine with such a distinguished history. "Too oaky, too fruity, too soft: the very model of a modern Napa Cabernet," my tasting notes say for the most recent vintage. Perhaps the recent arrival of Marcus Notaro from Col Solare (another Ste. Michelle property) will change things.

Staglin Family Vineyard

1570 Bella Oaks Ln, Rutherford, CA 94573

(1) 707 944 0477

www.staglinfamily.com

Napa Valley

Oakville, Salus, Cabernet Sauvignon

61 acres

Staglin is one of the wave of wineries founded in the 1980s by people who had been successful elsewhere and decided they wanted to make wine. The vineyard is in a historic situation and was part of Beaulieu (contributing to the Georges de Latour Private Reserve) until the Staglins purchased it. In 2015 they shared a purchase of the adjacent Fahrig Ranch, which is planted with Cabernet Sauvignon. David Abreu manages the vineyards; Michel Rolland consults on winemaking. The winery is completely underground; the visitor center is in a historic house that was on the property and has been restored. The focus is on Cabernet Sauvignon and Chardonnay, with the top wines labeled simply as Staglin Family Estate. Salus is used to indicated a second label. The Cabernet Sauvignons usually include very small amounts of other Bordeaux varieties, but the general impression is full-force varietal, very intense and Californian. The Chardonnay is quite intense and extracted, with phenolics on the finish.

Viader Vineyards

1120 Deer Park Road, Deer Park, CA 94576

(1) 707 963 3816

tastings@viader.com

Delia Viader

www.viader.com

Napa Valley

Napa Valley

29 acres; 60,000 bottles

Viader Vineyards occupies a steep slope on Howell Mountain that runs down into Bell Canyon. It's at an elevation of 400 m, just below the Howell Mountain AVA. Purchased and then cleared in 1981, the land was planted with Cabernet Sauvignon, Cabernet Franc, and Petit Verdot. There's no Merlot or Malbec because they do not do well in the mountain environment. "I planted Petit Verdot thinking it would go into the Proprietary Red but it just didn't fit," says Delia Viader, explaining why Viader's blend is solely Cabernet Sauvignon and Cabernet Franc. "Differences between the wines are more vintage driven than by variety per se because I change the blend with the vintage," she says. Cabernet Sauvignon is always a majority, varying from 51-75% over the past decade. The Petit Verdot goes into a monovarietal wine, as does any Cabernet Franc that isn't used for the Proprietary Red; there's also a blended wine that is largely Cabernet Sauvignon and Syrah. Other wines are made from purchased fruit. A change in style may occur as Alex Viader takes over, as he prefers more intensity and extraction. The 2012 shows more power and intensity than previously, but retains that characteristic chocolaty smoothness coming from the Cabernet Franc, and making Viader a distinctive wine.

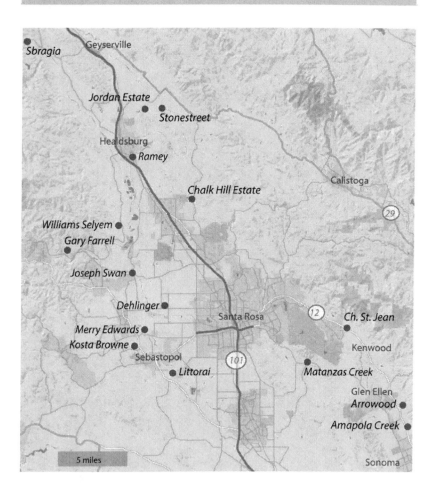

Amapola Creek

 392 London Way, Sonoma, CA 95476

📞 (1) 707 938 3783

@ david@amapolacreek.com

David DuBois

🌐 amapolacreek.com

Sonoma Valley

🍷 Cabernet Sauvignon

19 acres; 30,000 bottles

I was extremely careful not to arrive too early when I visited Richard Arrowood at his new winery, Amapola Creek, just below the Monte Rosso vineyard. During a visit to Monte Rosso earlier, the crew had mentioned that Richard was a well known gun collector, and I was anxious not to be treated as a trespasser. I arrived to be greeted by Richard with his arm in a sling; he had had an accident when requalifying for his concealed gun permit. Richard Arrowood is a legendary winemaker. He started at Chateau St. Jean, where he stayed from 1974 to 1990, when he left to run his own winery, the eponymous Arrowood, which he had started in 1986. After Arrowood was sold to Mondavi, and then changed hands multiple times following Constellation's purchase of Mondavi, Richard moved on to another winery, Amapola Creek. He had bought the site and planted a vineyard in 2000, with the intention of selling grapes, but decided when he left Arrowood to make the wine himself. With the same red volcanic soils as the Monte Rosso Vineyard, Amapola Creek is a 40 ha ranch on the western slopes of the mountain; the 8 ha of vineyards are planted with French clones of Cabernet Sauvignon and a little Petit Verdot, Syrah, and Grenache. Around 85-90% of production is red. The first Cabernet Sauvignon vintage in 2005 was 100% varietal; in 2006 and 2007, a little Petit Verdot was included. The Cabernet is a blend of four different vineyard plots. The most promising vintage in my tasting was the 2006.

Arrowood Winery ★★

14347 Sonoma Highway, Glen Ellen, CA 95442

(1) 707 938 5170

hospitality@arrowoodvineyards.com

www.arrowoodvineyards.com

Sonoma Valley

Reserve Speciale

19 acres; 250,000 bottles

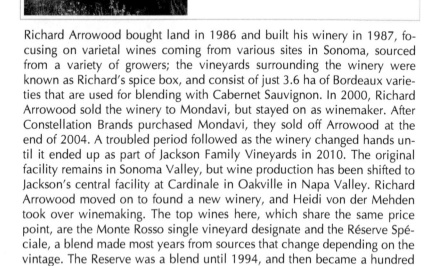

Richard Arrowood bought land in 1986 and built his winery in 1987, focusing on varietal wines coming from various sites in Sonoma, sourced from a variety of growers; the vineyards surrounding the winery were known as Richard's spice box, and consist of just 3.6 ha of Bordeaux varieties that are used for blending with Cabernet Sauvignon. In 2000, Richard Arrowood sold the winery to Mondavi, but stayed on as winemaker. After Constellation Brands purchased Mondavi, they sold off Arrowood at the end of 2004. A troubled period followed as the winery changed hands until it ended up as part of Jackson Family Vineyards in 2010. The original facility remains in Sonoma Valley, but wine production has been shifted to Jackson's central facility at Cardinale in Oakville in Napa Valley. Richard Arrowood moved on to found a new winery, and Heidi von der Mehden took over winemaking. The top wines here, which share the same price point, are the Monte Rosso single vineyard designate and the Réserve Spéciale, a blend made most years from sources that change depending on the vintage. The Reserve was a blend until 1994, and then became a hundred percent Cabernet Sauvignon.

Chalk Hill Estate

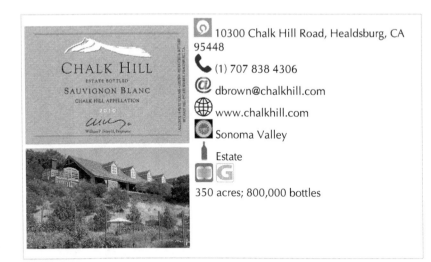

10300 Chalk Hill Road, Healdsburg, CA 95448

(1) 707 838 4306

dbrown@chalkhill.com

www.chalkhill.com

Sonoma Valley

Estate

350 acres; 800,000 bottles

The Chalk Hill Estate shows in microcosm the diversity of terroirs in this sub-AVA within Russian River Valley, going from warm, south-facing areas resembling Bordeaux to cool north-facing areas that resemble Alsace. "Bordeaux varieties only really ripen here in just the right sites, it's much cooler than Napa," says vineyard manager Mark Lingenfelder. Chalk Hill Estate was 50% Pinot Noir in the mid eighties, but the sites that are suitable for black grapes are really too warm for Pinot. The estate today is a mix of white varieties (mostly Chardonnay with a little Sauvignon Blanc) and Bordeaux varieties. The Cabernet is planted on the tops of warm south-facing slopes where the soil is based on red volcanic rocks. There is an unusually high concentration of the old varieties, mostly Malbec (9 ha), with a little Carmenère (1 ha). This has led to the production of some unusual blends, Cabernet/Malbec, Cabernet/Carmenère, Merlot/Malbec, and a Cabernet/Petit Verdot named for the new proprietor, W. P Foley, who purchased Chalk Hill in 2010. The estate wine used to be labeled as Cabernet Sauvignon, but lost the varietal label when the proportion of Cabernet fell below 75% as the result of planting more Malbec. Judging from the massive character and very high alcohol levels of the wines, you would never guess that this was a relatively cool climate for Cabernet. It wasn't really clear to me whether the difference between the relatively open Cabernet/Carmenère and the somewhat closed Cabernet/Malbec was due to the minor variety (20% Carmenère or 10% Malbec) or the source of the Cabernet Sauvignon, as I had not expected the Malbec to bring so much more structure than the Carmenère.

Dehlinger Winery *

4101 Vine Hill Road, Sebastopol, CA 95472

(1) 707 823 2378

www.dehlingerwinery.com

Sonoma Valley

Russian River Valley, Cabernet Sauvignon

Tom Dehlinger studied winemaking and viticulture at Davis in 1970; he thought he would make wine as a hobby, but it took over. The vineyard was a pioneering effort. "I bought this parcel in 1973 and planted the first 14 acres in 1975 with the best varieties of the time, Pinot Noir, Chardonnay, Gewürztraminer, Riesling. The Riesling was regrafted to Chardonnay a year later. Two acres of Cabernet were planted using a virus free clone in 1975, on AxR1 like all the others," he recollects. "We started our second planting with 3.5 acres of Cabernet Franc, we planted 5 more acres of Cabernet Sauvignon, and in 1988 we planted 3 acres of Merlot. The experiment was partly successful and partly unsuccessful. The Cabernet Franc and Merlot were planted adjacent to the Cabernet Sauvignon in slightly lower areas; the problem was that the areas were not optimally drained, so I don't think we have given Cabernet Franc and Merlot the best shot that they could have in this area." At first the Cabernet Sauvignon was vinified as a monovarietal wine, there were Cabernet Sauvignon-Merlot blends between 1992 and 1997 (the Cabernet Franc was too herbal to be included), and since 1998 the Cabernet Sauvignon has been a monovarietal. Today there are two bottlings of Cabernet Sauvignon; varietal-labeled from the best areas, and since 2002 a Claret from the lesser areas. My favorite was the Bordeaux blend from 1995.

Gary Farrell Wines

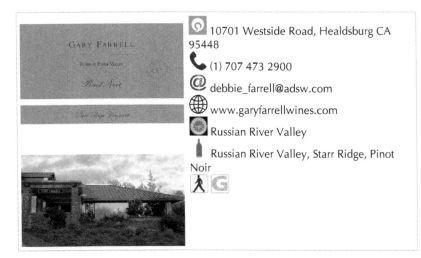

10701 Westside Road, Healdsburg CA 95448

(1) 707 473 2900

debbie_farrell@adsw.com

www.garyfarrellwines.com

Russian River Valley

Russian River Valley, Starr Ridge, Pinot Noir

Gary Farrell became involved in winemaking in the Russian River Valley in the 1970s and began to make his own wine in 1982. The model was based on purchasing fruit from top vineyard sites, including Rochioli and the adjacent Allen vineyard. A winery was built in 2000 in a beautiful location overlooking Westside Road with a spectacular view of the area. It was sold to Allied Domecq in 2004 and now is in the hands of Beam Wine Estates. Gary Farrell left in 2009 to start an-other winery. Currently the winery produces 4,000 cases of Russian River Valley selection, 1,000 cases from Carneros fruit from sister company Buena Vista, and 2,400 cases of single vineyard Pinot Noirs. Typically Pinot Noir is about 60% of production and Chardonnay about 30%. Winemaker Susan Reed says that they want the wines to be fruit driven so they pick a little earlier than most in order to get lower alcohol. They want people to be able to tell the wines are Gary Farrell. There is complete destemming, 5-7 days cold soak, and fermentation until pressing off at 1 degree Brix; all the press wine usually goes into the Russian River Valley bottling. This gets 30% new oak, and the single vineyard wines get 40%. Of the Russian River wines in this tasting, Hallberg is a bigger, darker wine, with black, richer fruits (partly reflecting the Dijon clones), whereas Rochioli and Allen vineyards are all about finesse, leaner with higher acidity and more purity of line.

Jordan Vineyard & Winery

1474 Alexander Road, Healdsburg, CA 95448

(1) 800 654 1213

lmattson@jordanwinery.com

Lisa Mattson

www.jordanwinery.com

Alexander Valley

Jordan

111 acres; 1,200,000 bottles

Jordan has followed an unusual course of development, moving from 100% Estate wine in 1990 to 2% today. "Tom Jordan wanted to make wine in the style of Bordeaux. He thought that what separated the first growths was that they owned their own vineyards, but the tenor of the time was that soil wasn't important, you just put in the right cultivar for the degree days," says winemaker Rob Davis, who has been in charge of every vintage since the inaugural 1976. Phylloxera forced replanting after 1990, but many of the vineyard blocks have been abandoned or the grapes sold off. Today most of the fruit for Jordan's wines comes from around twenty growers, many located in Geyserville. The Jordan Cabernet Sauvignon is usually at the limit for varietal labeling (75% Cabernet Sauvignon), with Merlot as the second component, and then about 4-7% Petit Verdot and 1% Malbec. A mixture of French and American oak is used for maturation. The wines are intended to be drinkable on release—an important aspect being that Jordan has a major presence in restaurants—and the style is best described by Rob Davis: "I like fruit," but these tend to elegance rather than power, and there's a firm policy of keeping to moderate alcohol levels (recent vintages are all stated at 13.5%). The wines seem to alternate between richer, heavier vintages in New World style (2008, 2006, 2003) and more elegant vintages in more European style (2007, 2004, 1990).

Joseph Swan Vineyards

2916 Laguna Road, Forestville CA 95436

(1) 707 573 3747

rod@swanwinery.com

Rod Berglund

www.swanwinery.com

Sonoma County

Trenton Estate Vineyard, Pinot Noir

Joseph Swan started his vineyard by purchasing a small farm in Russian River Valley in 1967. There was some Zinfandel on the farm, but new plantings focused on Pinot Noir and Chardonnay. Rod Berglund joined the winery in 1979, and runs it today together with his wife Lynn, Joe Swan's daughter. Rod was part of a group of winemakers who tried to define the typicity of Pinot Noir in Russian River Valley. It was perhaps too early because they did not reach agreement, he explains. "Swan produces Pinot Noir from several sites all of which are different. I think site triumphs all else. I like working with a multiplicity of clones because that gives a more complex wine," he says. The winery is focused on Pinot Noir; its proportion of production varies with the year , but is usually around 50-60%. Although the Swan selection of Pinot Noir is a famous clone in California, Joe Swan began grafting over to Dijon clones (or other selections from Burgundy), because he thought they gave better results. There are four bottlings of Pinot Noir; one comes from estate fruit and is matured in three quarters new oak, the others are matured in one third new oak. The Trenton Station Vineyard is part of the estate and makes a rather Burgundian Pinot Noir.

Kistler Vineyards

4707 Vine Hill Road, Sebastopol CA 95472

(1) 707 823 5603

mfbixler@kistlerwine.com

www.kistlerwine.com

Santa Cruz Mountains

Sonoma County, Les Noisetiers, Chardonnay

Steve Kistler and Marc Bixler met in 1974 and started the winery in 1979. "We are still doing it, which is not really true of most startup wineries. Usually the principals have either changed or they have hired other people to do the work," says Marc Bixler. Kistler makes wine from two different areas. There are several vineyards within 4 miles of the rather discrete winery which is identified only by the road number. The home vineyard is all chardonnay. The main Pinot Noir vineyards are about a mile or so north and south of the winery. Most are labeled as Sonoma Coast even if they are Russian River Valley. Many of their old vineyard bottlings were from grapes purchased from specific vineyards, but now they own all their own vineyards. "It's so difficult to grow we don't want to rely on others. Our style of Pinot Noir over rides regional specificities. We have a very specific style and it affects the methods we use. We want a very richly flavored style without too strong tannin influence. We don't do anything to eliminate tannins," says Marc. A change in tannin management really occurred in 2002, although there was a transition from 1999-2001. The change has made the wines easier to drink sooner, although that wasn't the major objective. New oak has been reduced from 100% to 80%. If anything, Kistler is better known for its Chardonnays—there are about 12 different Chardonnays compared to 5 Pinots—mostly from single vineyards. The blended wines are really a sort of second label to the single vineyard wines. Marc summarizes the style: "Kistler should have a powerful nose with fruit, some oak nut not too noticeable, a great deal of rich fruit in the mouth with lots of dark flavors, ripe but fresh not jammy or muddy."

Kosta Browne Winery ★★

1300 Montgomery Road, Sebastopol CA 95472

(1) 707 823 7430

dkosta@kostabrowne.com

Tony Lombardi

www.kostabrowne.com

Russian River Valley

Russian River Valley, Keefer, Pinot Noir

Kosta Browne began when Dan Kosta and Michael Browne, who were in the restaurant business, started by buying grapes and a barrel and made some wine. From one barrel (about 25 cases) they moved to 250 cases and then to 2,500 cases. They raised capital in 2001 and became professional. All their grapes are pur-chased. Kosta Browne is located in an old facility that used to be a center for handling apples in Sonoma. Other producers often refer to Kosta Browne wines as "big." They are felt to be high in alcohol and extract and to represent the forceful Californian style. But I can't say they entirely appear that way to me, although my tasting at Kosta Browne focused on barrel samples from different clones, oak, or means of vinification, rather than finished wines. Forceful to some extent, perhaps, but with balanced smooth palates emphasizing the fruits. Alcohol usually pushes close to 15%, which may be a problem in matching foods, and the supple tannins are subsumed by the fruits. These may well be wines to consume relatively early rather than to age. Tasting the current vintage in February 2011 confirmed the impression from the extensive barrel tastings that the style here is for precision, although the wines are at the richer end of the spectrum.

Littorai Wines

788 Gold Ridge Rd, Sebastopol, CA 95472

(1) 707 823 9586

info@littorai.com

Ted Lemon

www.littorai.com

Russian River Valley

Sonoma Coast, Hirsch Vineyard, Pinot Noir

Ted Lemon began Littorai in 1993 with just 300 cases of production. "When we started I did not have any interest in what I think of as the American flamboyant school of wine," he says, so the target was to sell to restaurants where a more elegant style might be better received. This now accounts for roughly two thirds of sales, the rest going to a mailing list. About 40% of production comes from estate vineyards, owned or on long term lease, the rest from purchased fruit. The estate vineyards stretch from the winery at the western edge of Russian River Valley to the Anderson Valley. Ted is an enthusiast for biodynamic viticulture. "We rejected organic viticulture because it substituted organic for synthetic but retained the basic idea of western agronomy," he says, adding that this is not so true of organic viticulture today. Littorai started to go biodynamic in 1998. Consisting of 12 hectares of farmland with about 10% planted to a Pinot Noir vineyard, the home estate will ultimately become completely self sufficient; all it lacks at the moment is a cow. Winemaking is as natural as possible, a major target being to avoid acidification. New oak is usually around 30% except for the two blended Pinots that are about 10%. The wines have an unusual elegance for the region.

Matanzas Creek Winery

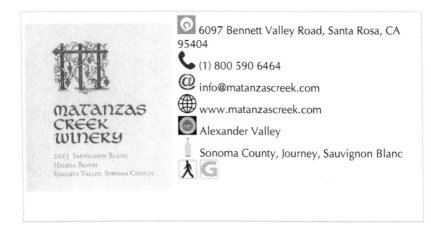

6097 Bennett Valley Road, Santa Rosa, CA 95404

(1) 800 590 6464

info@matanzascreek.com

www.matanzascreek.com

Alexander Valley

Sonoma County, Journey, Sauvignon Blanc

Matanzas Creek was there right at the start of the revival of winemaking on the North Coast, when it was established in 1977 in Bennett Valley to the east of Santa Rosa (long before Bennett Valley became an AVA). The location is a little off the beaten winery track in Sonoma. Originally a family winery, with wines made in an old barn, the property changed hands in 2000 when it was bought by Kendall-Jackson. Winemaking was moved to Jackson's larger facility at Stonestreet in 2010 to allow renovations at Matanzas Creek, and Marcia Monahan-Torres became the winemaker. There are varietal wines from Chardonnay, Sauvignon Blanc, and Merlot. Journey is used as the label for the top wines, and includes the same varietals as well as a blended red. There are several Sauvignon Blancs from different locations, two Chardonnays, and four bottlings of Merlot. Differences between the bottlings are carefully cultivated— Marcia selects yeasts for fermentation according to the property of each batch of grapes, for example—but Journey is more complete and complex in each case.

Merry Edwards Wines ★★

MERRY EDWARDS
2010
RUSSIAN RIVER VALLEY
PINOT NOIR
KLOPP RANCH
MÉTHODE À L'ANCIENNE
ALCOHOL 14.5% BY VOLUME

830 Denbe Saint Court, Suite B, Windsor, CA 95492

(1) 707 838 9950

merry@merryedwards.com

Merry Edwards

www.merryedwards.com

Russian River Valley

Russian River Valley, Olivet Lane, Pinot Noir

Merry Edwards is regarded as one of the pioneer winemakers in California. Her interest in Pinot Noir dates from her first winemaking position in 1974 at Mount Eden Vineyards in the Santa Cruz Mountains. From the plantings there she developed the Rae clone (now known as UCD 37), which is a major part of her own estate. As a Chardonnay specialist, she was the founding winemaker at Matanzas Creek in 1977. Her own winery was founded in 1997. Wines come from six estate vineyards and also from two vineyards under long-term acreage contracts allowing her to control viticulture. "We feel that farming is the only way to come to great Pinot and that is what we have based everything on," she says. In addition to the single vineyard wines, there is a Russian River bottling consisting of declassified lots. The Sonoma Coast bottling, which was made from purchased fruit, is being discontinued. The newest development is a Sauvignon Blanc, barrel fermented in the style of Fumé Blanc. Vinification for Pinot Noir follows the usual lines, al-though there's a little more use of new oak than average, running to around 55-60% in the regional blends and to 75-80% in the single vineyard designations. Describing her wines, she says, "I probably have two stylistic aims. I like the fruit to come through, I view this as the personality of the wine. And I like to see the texture come through."

Peter Michael

12400 Ida Clayton Road, Calistoga, CA 94515

(1) 707 942 4459

retail@petermichaelwinery.com

www.petermichaelwinery.com

Sonoma County

Knights Valley, Les Pavots

177 acres

Located about an hour north of Napa, although the address says Calistoga, the Peter Michael Winery is in Knight's Valley of Sonoma County. The winery dates from the purchase of 630 acres of volcanic terrain on the slopes of Mount St. Helena in 1982, with the stated objective of producing wines in European style to reflect the terroirs. Vineyard elevations vary from 300-600 m. Today there are 6 Chardonnays, 4 Pinot Noirs, 3 Cabernet blends, and 2 Sauvignon Blanc-Sémillon blends. The whites all come from vineyards in Knights Valley; two Chardonnays come from selection of specific barrels, the others all represent specific vineyards. Two Cabernets come from Knights Valley and the latest addition to the range, Au Paradis, comes from a vineyard that was recently purchased in Oakville, marking the winery's first venture into Napa. The Pinot Noirs all come from Fort Ross-Seaview in Sonoma County. Available only by subscription, with a waiting list, the wines have a fine reputation for understated elegance, but for my palate the power of the New World is evident. With alcohol levels of 14.5-15%, the Chardonnays make a powerful, oaky impression; the Sauvignon Blancs are unmistakably rich; and the reds have sweet, rich fruits. These are cult wines in California style.

Ramey Wine Cellars

202 Haydon St, Healdsburg, CA 95448

info@rameywine.com

www.rameywine.com reviews/ritchie.html

Sonoma Valley

Russian River, Chardonnay

David Ramey founded his own cellar in 1996 after making wines for several wineries in Sonoma and Napa. Most of the vineyards are in Russian River, and this is the basis for several single vineyard Chardonnays, which together with the Russian River Valley and Sonoma Coast bottlings are a major focus. There are also Pinot Noirs and Syrahs from Sonoma, and Cabernet Sauvignon from Napa. A second label called Sidebar has just been launched. The Ramey Chardonnays typify a more restrained Sonoma style (compared with the greater exuberance of Napa); the general Sonoma bottlings show more obvious evidence of oak than the single vineyards, where Ritchie Vineyard is the most subtle, and Hyde vineyard is more exotic and assertive. The Russian River Valley is a nice compromise. Among the reds I especially like Pedregal Vineyard Cabernet Sauvignon for its sense of precision. East-facing Rogers Creek vineyard in Sonoma produces a restrained Syrah along European lines; the west-facing Shanel vineyard produces more of a full-force New World expression of Syrah.

Sbragia Family Vineyards **★**

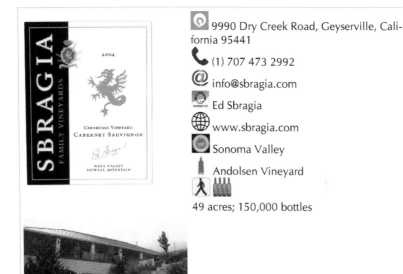

9990 Dry Creek Road, Geyserville, California 95441

(1) 707 473 2992

info@sbragia.com

Ed Sbragia

www.sbragia.com

Sonoma Valley

Andolsen Vineyard

49 acres; 150,000 bottles

Ed Sbragia grew up in Dry Creek Valley—"basically my heritage is Zinfandel and French Colombard," he says—got a chemistry degree from Davis, worked for Gallo, discovered wine, went back to school, worked for Foppiano for a year, and then went to Beringer for 32 years. He started his own production in 2001, while still at Beringer. His first release was in 2004. He purchased his present property in 2006. His own grapes are Sauvignon Blanc, Zinfandel, Chardonnay, Merlot; purchased grapes come from growers in Dry Creek and in Mayacamas mountains, and from two vineyards on Howell Mountain. All the Cabernets are single vineyard designates, with about 10 tons of grapes making 250 cases each. His son is the winemaker. The Sbragia winery is located in Sonoma, but most of his Cabernets come from Napa. This was an especially interesting tasting as the wines were all distinct, and it did not seem to me that there was any consistent difference between those from the Napa side and those from the Sonoma side of the Mayacamas mountains.

Chateau St. Jean

8555 Sonoma Highway, PO Box 293, Kenwood, CA 95452

(1) 707 833 4134

cs_chateaustjean@chateaustjean.com

Carrie Reed

www.chateaustjean.com

Sonoma Valley

Cinq Cepages

91 acres; 3,000,000 bottles

Founded in 1973, Chateau St. Jean was a pioneer for producing single vineyard designate wines. "The owners of Chateau St. Jean asked me to do vineyard designates like the Burgundians do," says Richard Arrowood, Chateau St. Jean's legendary first winemaker (who left in 1990). Chateau St. Jean was best known for its single vineyard Chardonnays, at one time as many as nine, although red wine was a major focus, with emphasis on Cabernet Sauvignon, until 1980. There was a pause in red wine production in the early eighties, and then it resumed with a blended wine based on Cabernet Sauvignon. When phylloxera forced replanting, the estate was about 80 ha, with about half planted, mostly with white varieties, but replanting focused on black varieties. "We were set on producing a blended wine, using all five Bordeaux varieties, which was close to impossible at the time," says current winemaker Margo Van Staaveren, who has been at Chateau St. Jean for thirty years, and saw the ownership change when it was sold to Beringer in 1996. 1990 was the first vintage of Cinq Cepages. "Cabernet Sauvignon has varied from 75-83%; the next most frequent variety is usually Merlot today, although previously it was Cabernet Franc.

Malbec and Petit Verdot are used in small amounts because they have such varietal expression that otherwise they would dominate the blend," she says. About half of the grapes comes from vineyards owned by Chateau St. Jean, but outside the home estate, so sources may include Sonoma Valley, Alexander Valley, Knights Valley, Dry Creek Valley, and Russian River Valley, depending on the year. Until 2007, the wine carried a varietal label as Cabernet Sauvignon, but that was removed as of 2008. "This had been the intent from the beginning. We put Cabernet Sauvignon on the label at the beginning because we were so closely identified with white wine," Margo says.

Stonestreet

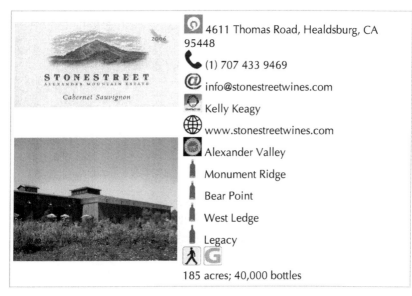

4611 Thomas Road, Healdsburg, CA 95448

(1) 707 433 9469

info@stonestreetwines.com

Kelly Keagy

www.stonestreetwines.com

Alexander Valley

Monument Ridge

Bear Point

West Ledge

Legacy

185 acres; 40,000 bottles

Stonestreet was created by Jesse Jackson, who started in wine by purchasing an orchard of pear and walnut trees in Lakeport (in the Central Valley) and converting it to a vineyard for Chardonnay production. He purchased a mountain estate in Sonoma's Alexander Valley in 1995 and turned it into a brand for Cabernet Sauvignon and Chardonnay. (Stonestreet was his middle name.) Stonestreet has 3,200 ha with 350 ha planted, including 200 ha of Cabernet Sauvignon. The vineyards are largely on the mountain slopes, where 80 ha had been planted in 1982, another 80 ha in 1991, more by Jackson after the acquisition in 1995, and then again in 2005. The overall balance of production is 80% red. Stonestreet is part of Jackson Family Vineyards, and while some of the grapes are used for its own bottlings, some are used by other vineyards in the group. The Stonestreet facility is also used to make wine for other properties in the group. Cabernet tends to be grown on higher plots on the mountains, because an inversion layer of cold air lower down makes ripening difficult. A series of monovarietal Cabernet Sauvignons come from single vineyards, Bear Point (below the fog line at 400 m), West Ledge (within the fog line at 550 m), and Monolith and Christopher (above the fog line at 700 m and 800 m). Monument Ridge is a bottling from sites all across the property. Legacy is an Alexander Valley blend that includes lots from the valley floor. "Mountain sites give far more variability in growth and ripening than on the flat.

New plantings of Merlot, Petit Verdot, and Malbec are going very well; but blending them in would cause loss of site specificity," says winemaker Graham Weerts. The Stonestreet wines are not wines for immediate gratification, which has been a marketing problem in the past. They have been trying to make the wines a little rounder and more opulent.

 6575 Westside Road, Healdsburg, CA 95448

📞 (1) 707 433 6425

@ contact@williams-selyem.com

Bob Cabral

🌐 www.williams-selyem.com

Russian River Valley

🍾 Sonoma County, Rochioli Riverblock, Pinot Noir

Williams Selyem is one of the standard bearers for Russian River Valley, and one of the few original pioneers still to remain independent. Started by Ed Selyem and Burt Williams, who had been amateur winemakers, the first vintage was made in a two-car garage in 1981; the original name of Hacienda del Rio was changed to Williams Selyem in 1984. Burt Williams made the vintages through 1997, when the winery was sold to John and Kathe Dyson, after which Bob Cabral took over as winemaker, making all the wines until leaving in 2015. Production functioned out of what was virtually a trailer park until 2010, when a splendid new winery was built at the top of the hill. Pinot Noir is about 85% of production. Wines range from the Central Coast, Sonoma County, and Russian River Valley appellation bottlings to an impressive series of single vineyard wines from top sites, including the 30 ha of estate vineyards. Winemaking is straightforward, with 20-25% use of whole clusters, five day cold soak, and addition of Williams Selyem's own strain of yeast to start fermentation. "It's very cookbook winemaking" says Bob Cabral. "Whether I'm making a $30 or $100 Pinot, the only real variable will be the proportion of new oak, from 40-80%." Appellation wines get bottled in August and the single vineyards after Christmas. There is no fining or filtration. One legacy of Williams' winemaking is the use of low sulfur levels (10-15 ppm), as Burt was allergic to sulfur. More than 90% of the single vineyard production sells to the mailing list, so the wines can be hard to find.

Saintsbury

📍 1500 Los Carneros Ave, Napa, CA 94559

📞 (1) 707 252 0592

@ info@saintsbury.com

👤 Richard Ward

🌐 www.saintsbury.com

Carneros

Carneros, Lees Vineyard, Pinot Noir

Saintsbury was established in 1981 when Dick Ward and David Graves, who met at oenology classes at UC Davis, decided on Carneros for their vineyard because of its history with Pinot Noir. They have always purchased most of their fruit, although they grow a higher percentage of Pinot Noir than other varieties. Their own vineyards are the home ranch, the RMS vineyard just down the road, and the Brown Ranch, which comprise 12 ha of the total 21 ha from which they source grapes. They have control of the viticulture at vineyards where they buy grapes. In 1983 it became apparent that individual vineyards varied differently in each vintage so they split production into regular production and the "Garnet" value bottlings intended for early drinking. The distinction was based on selection. However, the Garnet label was sold to Silverado Cellars in 2011. In 1990 they started to make a Reserve Pinot Noir, then they moved to single vineyard bottlings in 2004. Grapes are destemmed, there is cold soak for a few days, followed by a mix of natural and inoculated fermentation. Blends use 15-25% new oak; the single vineyard wines use 30-40% new oak. All of the appellation blends are under 14% alcohol; the single vineyards are under 14.5%. Single vineyard wines are about 10% of total production, which is around 45,000 cases. A vertical tasting gave a very good sense of aging potential. The wines reach a turning point with sous bois showing within a decade, but then they continue to develop beautifully and slowly for another decade.

The Donum Estate

1160 Hopper Ave, Santa Rosa, CA 95403

(1) 707 939 2290

lhandley@thedonumestate.com

Anne Moller Racke

www.thedonumestate.com

Carneros

Carneros, Pinot Noir

The Donum Estate was created in 2001. Previously it had been part of the Buena Vista Carneros vineyards, but when the Moller Racke family sold Buena Vista to Allied Domecq, 80 ha of the 400 ha of vineyards were split off to form the Donum Estate. These include 28 ha in the old Tula Vista Ranch in Carneros, 8 ha of the well known Ferguson Block a mile way, and another 4.5 ha of the Nugent Ranch in Russian River. There are 56 ha altogether, almost all planted with Pinot Noir; there is just a little Chardonnay. The vineyards were mostly planted in the late 1980s and 1990s at a time when there was more emphasis on rootstocks than clones. Plantings include a clone obtained from Roederer Estate in Anderson Valley, but it seems to be distinct from the clones that Roederer uses for sparkling wine production, as it has small berries with thick skins that produce dark wines. This is now known as the Donum clone. Some vineyards were grafted over to Dijon clones in 2001 and 2004. The headquarters for vineyard operations are on the Carneros ranch, but wine is made at a custom crush facility in Russian River. There are two labels: Donum Estate itself and also Robert Stemmler, which mostly represent different vineyard blocks, but with some barrel selection. When Donum started, they made only one wine, but then decided to move to single vineyard designations. Presently there are 6 different Pinots under the Donum label and 3 under Stemmler, with a total production around 8,000 cases. "I have been thinking about stylistic aims because we get blame because the wines are so intense. They are vineyard-driven more than by winemaking techniques. I do like wines with concentration, but I do not want to lose delicacy," says Anne Moller Racke

Mount Eden Vineyards   **

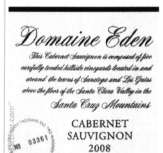

 22020 Mt. Eden Road, Saratoga, CA 95070-9729

 (888) 865-9463

 info@mounteden.com

Ellie Patterson

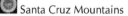 www.mounteden.com

 Santa Cruz Mountains

 Santa Cruz Mountains

12 acres; 18,000 bottles

Driving up a precipitous dirt track on the edge of the Santa Cruz Mountains to the Mount Eden Winery with a solid sheet of water descending from the sky, I began to wonder whether current owner and winemaker Jeffrey Patterson had been euphemistic when he warned me the track was 2.2 miles long. But the drive was worth it. The Mount Eden Winery was originally the Martin Ray winery, created in the 1940s after Martin Ray had bought and then later sold the nearby Paul Masson winery. After Martin Ray left in 1970, this became the Mount Eden winery in 1972. There were several rapid changes in winemaker, until Jeffrey Patterson started making the wine in 1981. The winery is perched at a height of about 700 m, overlooking Santa Clara Valley; on a clear day you can see to the Pacific, 14 miles away. Mount Eden produces Cabernet Sauvignon, Pinot Noir, and Chardonnay, a clear indication that this is cool climate for Cabernet Sauvignon. The Estate Cabernet Sauvignon is a Bordeaux-like blend, usually with about 75% Cabernet Sauvignon. Until 2000, when the vines had to be replanted because they had finally stopped producing, there was also a bottling of an Old Vines Cabernet Sauvignon, a 100% selection of a plot of Cabernet planted on its own roots by Martin Ray in the 1950s.

RIDGE 2010
MONTE BELLO®

MONTE BELLO VINEYARD   74% CABERNET SAUVIGNON,
20% MERLOT, 4% PETIT VERDOT, 2% CABERNET FRANC
SANTA CRUZ MOUNTAINS   13.2% ALCOHOL BY VOLUME
GROWN, PRODUCED & BOTTLED BY RIDGE VINEYARDS
18100 MONTE BELLO ROAD, P. O. BOX 1810, CUPERTINO, CA 95015

 17100 Monte Bello Road, Cupertino, CA 95014

📞 (408) 867 3233

@ wine@ridgewine.com

Paul Draper

🌐 www.ridgewine.com

Santa Cruz Mountains

Montebello

Geyserville

523 acres; 1,000,000 bottles

The first vineyards and original Monte Bello Winery in the Santa Cruz mountains date from 1885. Ridge Vineyards was established in 1959 by a group of scientists from the Stanford Research Institute, who made the wine. Paul Draper came to Ridge in 1969. He tasted the 1962 and 1964 (both monovarietal Cabernets) and was impressed: "It was the first time I tasted California wine outside of the old Inglenook and Beaulieu wines with the complexity of Bordeaux. Those two wines were the reason why I joined Ridge." He became the managing partner and winemaker. The company was sold to a Japanese pharmaceutical company in 1987, but this does not seem to have made any difference. From the estate, extended along the ridge since the original purchase, come the famous Monte Bello Cabernet Sauvignon and Chardonnay. Ridge is also famous for its single vineyard series of Zinfandels, which come from a wide range of locations, extending from Lytton Springs, Geyserville, and other vineyards in Sonoma, to a ranch in Paso Robles. Grapes come from both estate and purchased sources. At the Monte Bello estate, 24 parcels are usually used for producing the Monte Bello Cabernet, and another 21 for the Estate Cabernet. There are about 42 ha of vineyards for the black varieties altogether. The Estate Cabernet is essentially a second wine, although each parcel—or sometimes half parcel—is assessed separately. Decisions are made on most parcels before an initial assemblage, but some are left to be reassessed later, and one or two parcels change destination each year. The approach is distinctly Bordelais, with a perspective of viewing lots as more important than varieties. Paul shows some disdain for the modern style of full-blown Cabernets, and Monte Bello remains a classic: it's a long-lived wine, and Paul thinks it begin to show its characteristics around 9-12 years, developing until 20 or 30 years.

Thomas Fogarty Winery

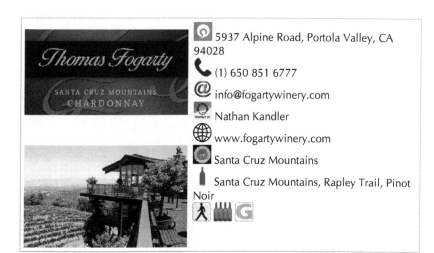

⊙ 5937 Alpine Road, Portola Valley, CA 94028

📞 (1) 650 851 6777

@ info@fogartywinery.com

👤 Nathan Kandler

🌐 www.fogartywinery.com

🔲 Santa Cruz Mountains

🍾 Santa Cruz Mountains, Rapley Trail, Pinot Noir

The eponymous Thomas Fogarty (a surgeon at Stanford) owned this land before he decided to make wine. The vineyards were planted in 1978 and Michael Martella came as the winemaker in 1981. The location has spectacular views all the way out to San Francisco Bay, at a sufficient elevation that you see the blimp cruising along below. Except for one vineyard that is being replanted, all are still the original plantings. The vines came from the David Bruce vineyard or the Martini selection, and have since been supplemented with some Dijon and Swan clones. Originally the best selections went into a Reserve bottling, but Fogarty moved to single vineyard bottling in 2002. Around the winery all the vineyards are planted to Pinot Noir or Chardonnay; there are some Bordeaux varieties at another vineyard 20 minutes farther south. The major Pinot Noir vineyards are Windy Hill (right beside the winery) which is presently being replanted, and Rapley Trail. The 2 ha of the Rapley Trail vineyard are the only areas with clay in the soil (heavier at the top, thinner below); the rest is loam and sand. The Rapley Trail vineyard has now been subdivided into blocks, with the inventive names of M for the middle and B for the bottom; it is picked from bottom to top over a one month period.

Mount Harlan

Mount Harlan

Calera Wine Company ***

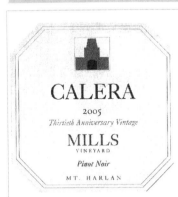

11300 Cienega Road, Hollister, CA 95023

(1) 831 637 9170

info@calerawine.com

Josh Jensen

www.calerawine.com

Mount Harlan

Mount Harlan, Mills Vineyard, Pinot Noir

Calera is sui generis. There is no other vineyard within fifty miles, there probably isn't any other vineyard in California at such a high elevation, and certainly there is none with limestone soils. The six vineyards of Pinot Noir total 36 ha; there are another 7 ha of Chardonnay and Viognier. Estate fruit is used for the single vine-yards and Mount Harlan cuvée; purchased fruit is the basis of the Central Coast bottling. The winery (much lower down the mountain than the vineyards them-selves) was converted from an old rock-crushing facility. Before a recent makeover, it was famous as one of the ugliest wineries around. It now houses a multi-storey gravity-fed winemaking facility (with a tasting room at one end for fans who make the pilgrimage up the mountain). Winemaking follows conventional Burgundian principles; the single vineyard wines spend 16 months in oak, 30% of which is new for most vineyards in most vintages. Vineyard differences were the most distinct in the current vintage. In older vintages, south-facing Mills consistently gave rounder wine than north-facing Reed, except for 2002, which seems to be the vintage in which both wines showed best, identifying the peak age as just under ten years. A certain lack of differentiation in flavor between them may reflect the high use of whole clusters for these lighter wines.

Index of Estates By Rating

3 star
Bryant Family Vineyard
Calera Wine Company
Harlan Estate
Opus One
Ridge Vineyards
Screaming Eagle Winery

2 star
Abreu Vineyards
Araujo Estate
Arrowood Winery
Caymus Vineyards
Chappellet Vineyard
Colgin Cellars
Corison Winery
Diamond Creek
Dominus Estate
Dunn Vineyards
Heitz Cellars
Joseph Phelps Vineyards
Kosta Browne Winery
Louis Martini Winery
Merry Edwards Wines
Chateau Montelena
Mount Eden Vineyards
Pride Mountain Vineyards
Robert Foley
Sbragia Family Vineyards
Schrader Cellars
Shafer Vineyards
Williams Selyem

1 star
Amapola Creek
Bell Wine Cellars
Chalk Hill Estate
Dehlinger Winery
Domaine Chandon Winery
The Donum Estate
Far Niente
Gary Farrell Wines
Grgich Hills Cellar
Groth Vineyards & Winery
Inglenook
Jarvis Winery
Jordan Vineyard & Winery
Joseph Swan Vineyards
Kistler Vineyards
Littorai Wines
Matanzas Creek Winery
Peter Michael
Philip Togni Vineyard
Ramey Wine Cellars
Robert Mondavi Winery
Robert Sinskey Vineyards
Saintsbury
Spottswoode Estate Vineyard
Chateau St. Jean
Stag's Leap Wine Cellars
Staglin Family Vineyard
Stonestreet
Thomas Fogarty Winery
Viader Vineyards

Alphabetical Index of Estates

Kosta Browne Winery	117
Littorai Wines	118
Louis Martini Winery	86
Matanzas Creek Winery	119
Merry Edwards Wines	120
Chateau Montelena	88
Mount Eden Vineyards	132
Opus One	90
Peter Michael	121
Philip Togni Vineyard	92
Pride Mountain Vineyards	93
Ramey Wine Cellars	122
Ridge Vineyards	134
Robert Foley	95
Robert Mondavi Winery	96
Robert Sinskey Vineyards	98
Saintsbury	130
Sbragia Family Vineyards	123
Schrader Cellars	99
Screaming Eagle Winery	100
Shafer Vineyards	102
Spottswoode Estate Vineyard	103
Chateau St. Jean	124
Stag's Leap Wine Cellars	104
Staglin Family Vineyard	106
Stonestreet	126
The Donum Estate	131
Thomas Fogarty Winery	136
Viader Vineyards	107
Williams Selyem	128

INTELLIGENT GUIDES TO WINES & TOP VINEYARDS

WINES OF FRANCE SERIES

WINE OF EUROPE SERIES

NEW WORLD WINE SERIES

BOOKS by Benjamin Lewin MW

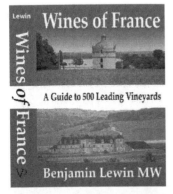

Wines of France

This comprehensive account of the vineyards and wines of France today is extensively illustrated with photographs and maps of each wine-producing area. Leading vineyards and winemakers are profiled in detail, with suggestions for wines to try and vineyards to visit.

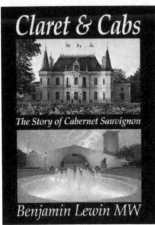

Claret & Cabs:
the Story of Cabernet Sauvignon

This worldwide survey of Cabernet Sauvignon and its blends extends from Bordeaux through the New World, defines the character of the wine from each region, and profiles leading producers.

In Search of Pinot Noir

Pinot Noir is a uniquely challenging grape with an unrivalled ability to reflect the character of the site where it grows. This world wide survey of everywhere Pinot Noir is grown extends from Burgundy to the New World, and profiles leading producers.

Wine Myths and Reality

Extensively illustrated with photographs, maps, and charts, this behind-the-scenes view of winemaking reveals the truth about what goes into a bottle of wine. Its approachable and entertaining style immediately engages the reader in the wine universe.